Fodor's®

Pocket
Santa Fe
& Taos

Excerpted from *Fodor's New Mexico*

Fodor's Travel Publications, Inc.
New York • Toronto • London • Sydney • Auckland
www.fodors.com

II

Fodor's Pocket Santa Fe & Taos

EDITORS: Daniel Mangin and Stephanie J. Adler

Editorial Contributors: Jeffrey Boswell, David Brown, Marilyn Haddrill, Christina Knight, M. T. Schwartzman (Essential Information editor), Heidi Sarna, Helayne Schiff, Nancy Zimmerman

Editorial Production: Stacey Kulig

Maps: David Lindroth, *cartographer*; Steven K. Amsterdam, Robert Blake, *map editors*

Design: Fabrizio La Rocca, *creative director*; Guido Caroti, *associate art director*; Lyndell Brookhouse-Gil, *cover design*; Jolie Novak, *photo editor*

Production/Manufacturing: Mike Costa

Cover Photograph: Buddy Mays/Corbis

Copyright

First Edition

ISBN 0–679–00306–1

Special Sales

Fodor's Travel Publications are available at special discounts for bulk purchases for sales promotions or premiums. Special editions, including personalized covers, excerpts of existing guides, and corporate imprints, can be created in large quantities for special needs. For more information, contact your local bookseller or write to Special Markets, Fodor's Travel Publications, 201 East 50th Street, New York, NY 10022. Inquiries from Canada should be directed to your local Canadian bookseller or sent to Random House of Canada, Ltd., Marketing Department, 2775 Matheson Boulevard East, Mississauga, Ontario L4W 4P7. Inquiries from the United Kingdom should be sent to Fodor's Travel Publications, 20 Vauxhall Bridge Road, London SW1V 2SA, England.

PRINTED IN THE UNITED STATES OF AMERICA

10 9 8 7 6 5 4 3 2 1

CONTENTS

Maps

ON THE ROAD WITH FODOR'S

WHEN I PLAN a vacation, the first thing I do is cast around among my friends and colleagues to find someone who's just been where I'm going. That's because there's no substitute for a recommendation from a good friend who knows your tastes, your budget, and your circumstances, someone who's just been there. Unfortunately, such friends are few and far between. So it's nice to know that there's *Fodor's Pocket Santa Fe & Taos*.

In the first place, this book won't stay home when you hit the road. It will accompany you every step of the way, steering you away from wrong turns and wrong choices and never expecting a thing in return. Most important of all, it's written and assiduously updated by the kind of people you *would* hit up for travel tips if you knew them. They're as choosy as your pickiest friend, and they're equipped with an insider's knowledge of Santa Fe and Taos. In these pages, they don't send you chasing down every sight in these two cities but have instead selected the best ones, the ones that are worthy of your time and money. Will this be the vacation of your dreams? We hope so.

About Our Writers

Our success in helping to make your trip the best of all possible vacations is a credit to the hard work of our extraordinary contributors.

Marilyn Haddrill, who updated the Essential Information section of this book and Chapter 1, is a veritable fountain of practical information about the entire state. Her wildest experience while on assignment? Trying to drive through a herd of hungry, bleating sheep to investigate a remote ranch.

Nancy Zimmerman, updater of the Santa Fe and Taos chapters, is a freelance writer, editor, and translator based in Tesuque, a village outside Santa Fe.

Connections

We're pleased that the American Society of Travel Agents continues to endorse Fodor's as its guidebook of choice. ASTA is the world's largest and most influential travel trade association, operating in more than 170 countries, with 27,000 members pledged to adhere to a strict code of ethics reflecting the Society's motto, "Integrity in Travel." ASTA shares Fodor's devotion to providing smart, honest travel information and advice to travelers, and we've long recommended that our readers—even those who have guidebooks and traveling friends—consult ASTA member agents for the experience and professionalism they bring to your vacation planning.

On Fodor's Web site (www.fodors.com), check out the Resource Center, an on-line companion to the Essential Information section of this book, complete with useful hot links to related sites. In our forums, you can also get lively advice from other travelers and more great tips from Fodor's experts worldwide.

How to Use This Book

Organization

Up front is Essential Information, an easy-to-use section arranged alphabetically by topic. Under each listing you'll find tips and information that will help you accomplish what you need to in Santa Fe and Taos. You'll also find addresses and telephone numbers of organizations and companies that offer destination-related services, information, and publications.

The first chapter, Destination: Santa Fe and Taos, helps get you in the mood for your trip. What's Where gets you oriented; New and Noteworthy cues you in on trends and happenings; Pleasures and Pastimes describes the activities and sights that make these cities unique; Fodor's Choice showcases our top picks.

Each chapter begins with an Exploring section, which is subdivided by neighborhood; each subsection recommends a walking or driving tour and lists sights in alphabetical order. Dining, Lodging, Nightlife and the Arts, Outdoor Activities and Sports, Shopping, and (in the Santa Fe chapter) Side Trips sections follow the exploring tours.

Icons and Symbols

★ Our special recommendations
✕ Restaurant
🏠 Lodging establishment
✕🏠 Lodging establishment whose restaurant warrants a special trip
🐣 Good for kids (rubber duck)
☞ Sends you to another section of the guide for more information
✉ Address
☎ Telephone number
🕐 Opening and closing times
💲 Admission prices (those we give apply to adults; substantially reduced fees are almost always available for children, students, and senior citizens)

Numbers in white and black circles (e.g., ③ ❸) that appear on the maps, in the margins, and within the tours correspond to one another.

Dining and Lodging

The restaurants and lodgings we list are the cream of the crop in each price range. Price charts appear in the Dining and Lodging sections in chapters 2 and 3.

Hotel Facilities

We always list the facilities that are available—but we don't specify whether you'll be charged extra to use them: When pricing accommodations, always ask what's included and assume that all rooms have private baths unless noted otherwise.

Assume that hotels operate on the European Plan (with no meals) unless we specify that they include breakfast or other meals in the rates.

Restaurant Reservations and Dress Codes

Reservations are always a good idea; we mention them only when they're essential or are not accepted. Unless otherwise noted, the restaurants listed are open daily for lunch and dinner.

Credit Cards

The following abbreviations are used: **AE,** American Express; **D,** Discover; **DC,** Diners Club; **MC,** MasterCard; and **V,** Visa.

Don't Forget to Write

You can use this book in the confidence that all prices and open-ing times are based on information supplied to us at press time; Fodor's cannot accept responsibility for any errors. Time inevitably brings changes, so always confirm information when it matters—especially if you're making a detour to visit a specific place.

Were the restaurants we recommended as described? Did our hotel picks exceed your expectations? Did you find a museum we recommended a waste of time? Keeping a travel guide fresh and up-to-date is a big job, and we welcome your feedback, positive *and* negative. If you have complaints, we'll look into them and revise our entries when the facts warrant it. If you've discovered a special place that we haven't included, we'll pass the information along to our correspondents and have them check it out. So send us your thoughts via e-mail at editors@fodors.com (specifying the name of the book on the subject line) or on paper in care of the New Mexico editor at Fodor's, 201 East 50th Street, New York, NY 10022. In the meantime, have a wonderful trip!

Karen Cure
Editorial Director

New Mexico

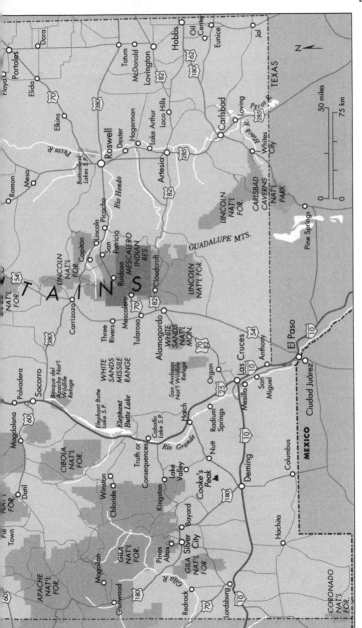

ESSENTIAL INFORMATION

Basic Information on Traveling in Santa Fe and Taos, Savvy Tips to Make Your Trip a Breeze, and Companies and Organizations to Contact

AIR TRAVEL

BOOKING YOUR FLIGHT

Price is only one factor to consider when booking a flight: frequency of service and even a carrier's safety record are often as important. Major airlines offer the greatest number of departures. Smaller airlines—including regional and no-frills airlines—usually have a limited number of flights daily. On the other hand, so-called low-cost airlines usually are cheaper, and their fares impose fewer restrictions, such as advance-purchase requirements. Safety-wise, low-cost carriers as a group have a good history—about equal to that of major carriers.

When you book, **look for nonstop flights** and **remember that "direct" flights stop at least once.** Try to **avoid connecting flights,** which require a change of plane. Two airlines may jointly operate a connecting flight, so ask if your airline operates every segment—you may find that your preferred carrier flies you only part of the way.

Ask your airline if it offers electronic ticketing, which eliminates all paperwork. There's no ticket to pick up or misplace. If you're not

checking baggage, you go directly to the gate and give the agent your confirmation number.

CARRIERS

➤ MAJOR AIRLINES: **American** (☎ 800/433–7300). **Continental** (☎ 800/525–0280). **Delta** (☎ 800/221–1212). **Northwest** (☎ 800/692–7000). **TWA** (☎ 800/221–2000). **United** (☎ 800/241–6522). **US Airways** (☎ 800/428–4322).

➤ SMALLER AIRLINES: **America West** (☎ 800/235–9292). **Frontier** (☎ 800/432–1359). **Mesa Air** (☎ 800/637–2247). **Reno Air** (☎ 800/736–6247). **Southwest** (☎ 800/435–9792).

➤ FROM THE U.K.: **British Airways** (☎ 0345/222111). **Delta** (☎ 0800/414767). **United Airlines** (☎ 0800/888555).

CUTTING COSTS

The least-expensive airfares to New Mexico are priced for round-trip travel and usually must be purchased in advance. To get the lowest airfare **check different routings.** Compare prices of flights to and from different airports if your destination or home city has more than one gateway. Also, price off-peak flights, which may be significantly less expensive.

When flying within the U.S., **plan to stay over a Saturday night** and **travel during the middle of the week** to get the lowest fare. These low fares are usually priced for round-trip travel and are nonrefundable. You can, however, change your return date for a fee ($75 on most major airlines).

Travel agents, especially those who specialize in finding the lowest fares (☞ Discounts & Deals, *below*), can be helpful when booking a plane ticket. When you're quoted a price, **ask your agent if the price is likely to get any lower.** Good agents know the seasonal fluctuations of airfares and can usually anticipate a sale or fare war. However, waiting can be risky: The fare could go *up* as seats become scarce, and you may wait so long that your preferred flight sells out. A wait-and-see strategy works best if your plans are flexible. If you must arrive and depart on certain dates, don't delay.

CHECK IN & BOARDING

Airlines routinely overbook planes, assuming that not everyone with a ticket will show up, but sometimes everyone does. When that happens, airlines ask for volunteers to give up their seats. In return these volunteers usually get a certificate for a free flight and are rebooked on the next flight out. If there are not enough volunteers, the airline must choose who will be denied boarding. The first to get bumped are passengers who checked in late and those flying on discounted tickets, so **get to the gate and check in as early as possible,** especially during peak periods.

Although the trend on international flights is to drop reconfirmation requirements, many airlines still ask you to reconfirm each leg of your international itinerary. Failure to do so may result in your reservation being canceled.

Always **bring a government-issued photo ID to the airport.** You may be asked to show it before you are allowed to check in.

ENJOYING THE FLIGHT

For more legroom **request an emergency-aisle seat.** Don't sit in the row in front of the emergency aisle or in front of a bulkhead, where seats may not recline.

If you don't like airline food, **ask for special meals when booking.** These can be vegetarian, low-cholesterol, or kosher, for example.

HOW TO COMPLAIN

If your baggage goes astray or your flight goes awry, complain right away. Most carriers require that you **file a claim immediately.**

➤ AIRLINE COMPLAINTS: U.S. Department of Transportation **Aviation Consumer Protection Division** (✉ C-75, Room 4107, Washington, DC 20590, ☎ 202/366–2220). **Federal Aviation**

Administration Consumer Hotline (☎ 800/322–7873).

AIRPORTS & TRANSFERS

The major gateway to New Mexico is Albuquerque International Sunport, 65 mi southwest of Santa Fe and 130 mi south of Taos. There is no regular air service between Albuquerque and Santa Fe.

➤ AIRPORT INFORMATION: **Albuquerque International Sunport** (⊠ Gibson Blvd. off I–25, 5 mi south of downtown, ☎ 505/842–4366). **Santa Fe Municipal Airport** (⊠ Airport Rd./NM 284 west of NM 14, ☎ 505/473–7243).

TRANSFERS

Shuttle buses operate between the Albuquerque International Sunport and Santa Fe and take about 1 hour and 20 minutes. The cost is about $20 each way. There's also a shuttle between Albuquerque's airport and Taos that takes about 2¾ hours and costs $35 each way. Reservations are advised on all shuttles. Ask about round-trip and group discounts.

➤ BETWEEN ALBUQUERQUE AND SANTA FE: **Shuttlejack** (☎ 505/982–4311).

➤ BETWEEN ALBUQUERQUE AND TAOS: **Faust Transportation** (☎ 505/758–7359).

BIKES IN FLIGHT

Most airlines will accommodate bikes as luggage, provided they are dismantled and put into a box. Call to see if your airline sells bike boxes (about $5; bike bags cost about $100), though you can often pick them up for free at bike shops. International travelers can sometimes substitute a bike for a piece of checked luggage for free; otherwise, it will cost about $100. U.S. and Canadian airlines charge a fee of $25 to $50.

BUS TRAVEL

Bus service is available between major cities and towns in New Mexico. A one-way ticket from Albuquerque to Santa Fe costs about $12; to Taos, about $22. One-way bus transport from Santa Fe to Taos costs about $20.

➤ BUS LINES: **Greyhound Albuquerque** (⊠ 300 2nd St. SW, ☎ 505/243–4435 or 800/231–2222). **Faust Transportation** (☞ Airports & Transfers, *above*). **Shuttlejack** (☞ Airports & Transfers, *above*).

BUSINESS HOURS

Banks generally are open in Santa Fe on weekdays between 9 and 3 and on Saturday between 9 and noon. In Taos they are open on weekdays between 9 and 5. Some branches are open between 10 and noon on Saturday.

Museums in Santa Fe and Taos are generally open daily from 9 or 10 AM to 5 or 6 PM, although hours may vary from season to season. Even during the summer, a peak travel time, some facilities close at 4 PM.

In Santa Fe the main post offices are open on weekdays from 8 to 5 (from 9 to 5 in Taos) and on Saturday between 9 and noon.

General business hours in New Mexico are between 9 and 5; most shops and galleries are open between 10 and 5 or 6, with limited hours on weekends. Store and commercial hours may vary from season to season (remaining open longer in summer than in winter).

CAMERAS & COMPUTERS

EQUIPMENT PRECAUTIONS

Always **keep your film, tape, or computer disks out of the sun.** Carry an extra supply of batteries, and **be prepared to turn on your camera, camcorder, or laptop** to prove to security personnel that the device is real. Always **ask for hand inspection of film,** which becomes clouded after successive exposure to airport X-ray machines, and **keep videotapes and computer disks away from metal detectors.**

ONLINE ON THE ROAD

Checking your e-mail or surfing the Web can sometimes be done in the business centers of major hotels, which usually charge an hourly rate. Web access is often available at fax and copy centers, many of which are open 24 hours daily including on weekends. Whether you have e-mail at home or not, you can **arrange to have a free e-mail address** from several services, including one available

at www.hotmail.com (the site explains how to apply for an address).

TRAVEL PHOTOGRAPHY

New Mexico is a superb spot for landscape and bird and wildlife photography. Many professional photographers use Kodachrome ASA 64, Fuji's Provia 100 and 200, or Velvia color slide film under all conditions, though you may want to pack a roll or two of higher-speed film, whether for slides or prints, to catch action shots. Be sure to pack extra batteries for your camera. A tripod is useful for almost any photography and highly recommended for photographing wildlife.

➤ PHOTO HELP: **Kodak Information Center** (☎ 800/242–2424). *Kodak Guide to Shooting Great Travel Pictures,* available in bookstores or from Fodor's Travel Publications (☎ 800/533–6478; $16.50 plus $4 shipping).

CAR RENTAL

Rates in Santa Fe begin at about $30 a day and $160 a week for an economy car with air-conditioning, an automatic transmission, and unlimited mileage. This does not include tax on car rentals, which is 10.75%, and a $2 per day surcharge. If you rent at the airport, there is an additional 2% tax.

➤ MAJOR AGENCIES: **Alamo** (☎ 800/327–9633, 0800/272–2000 in the U.K.). **Avis** (☎ 800/331–1212, 800/879–2847 in Canada).

Budget (☎ 800/527–0700, 0800/181181 in the U.K.). Dollar (☎ 800/800–4000; 0990/565656 in the U.K., where it is known as Eurodollar). Hertz (☎ 800/654–3131, 800/263–0600 in Canada, 0345/555888 in the U.K.). National InterRent (☎ 800/227–7368; 0345/222525 in the U.K., where it is known as Europcar InterRent).

➤ SMALLER AGENCIES: Sears (☎ 800/527–0770). Enterprise (☎ 800/322–8007). Pay-Less (☎ 800/541–1566). Rent Rite (☎ 800/554–7483). Rich Ford (☎ 800/331–3271). Thrifty (☎ 800/367–2277).

CUTTING COSTS

When pricing cars, **ask about the location of the rental lot.** Some off-airport locations offer lower rates, and their lots are only minutes from the terminal via complimentary shuttle. You also may want to **price local car-rental companies,** whose rates may be lower still, although their service and maintenance may not be as good as those of a name-brand agency. Remember to ask about required deposits, cancellation penalties, and drop-off charges if you're planning to pick up the car in one city and leave it in another.

Also **ask your travel agent about a company's customer-service record.** How has the company responded to late plane arrivals and vehicle mishaps? Are there often lines at the rental counter? If you're traveling during a holiday period, does a confirmed reservation guarantee you a car?

INSURANCE

When driving a rented car you are generally responsible for any damage to or loss of the vehicle. You also are liable for any property damage or personal injury that you may cause while driving. Before you rent, **see what coverage you already have** under the terms of your personal auto-insurance policy and credit cards.

For about $15 to $20 per day, rental companies sell protection, known as a collision- or loss-damage waiver (CDW or LDW), that eliminates your liability for damage to the car; it's always optional and should never be automatically added to your bill.

In most states you don't need a CDW if you have personal auto insurance or other liability insurance. However, **make sure you have enough coverage to pay for the car.** If you do not have auto insurance or an umbrella policy that covers damage to third parties, purchasing liability insurance and a CDW or LDW is highly recommended.

REQUIREMENTS

In New Mexico you must be 21 to rent a car, and rates may be higher if you're under 25. You'll pay extra for additional drivers (about

$2 per day), and for child seats (about $3 per day), which are compulsory for children under five. Non-U.S. residents will need a reservation voucher, a passport, a driver's license, and a travel policy that covers each driver, in order to pick up a car.

SURCHARGES

Before you pick up a car in one city and leave it in another, **ask about drop-off charges or one-way service fees,** which can be substantial. Note, too, that some rental agencies charge extra if you return the car before the time specified in your contract. To avoid a hefty refueling fee, **fill the tank right before you turn in the car,** but be aware that gas stations near the rental outlet may overcharge.

CAR TRAVEL

A car is the most convenient means of travel in New Mexico. Interstate 40 runs east–west across the middle of the state. Interstate 25 runs north from the state line at El Paso through Albuquerque and Santa Fe, then angles northeast to the Colorado line near Raton.

AUTO CLUBS

➤ IN CANADA: **Canadian Automobile Association** (CAA, ☎ 613/247–0117).

➤ IN THE U.K.: **Automobile Association** (AA, ☎ 0990/500–600), **Royal Automobile Club** (RAC,

☎ 0990/722722 for membership, 0345/121345 for insurance).

➤ IN THE U.S.: **American Automobile Association** (☎ 800/564–6222).

ROAD MAPS

The New Mexico Department of Tourism provides a detailed map of the state on request. GTR Mapping produces a topographical map of the state that depicts many backroads and recreational sites. The GTR maps are sold at convenience and grocery stores, bookstores, and department stores like Kmart and Wal-Mart.

➤ MAPS: **New Mexico Department of Tourism** (☎ 505/827–7400 or 800/545–2070). **GTR Mapping** (☎ 719/275–8948).

RULES OF THE ROAD

The speed limit along the interstates in much of New Mexico is 70 or 75 mph; it's 65 to 70 on U.S. highways (55 in more populated areas). In most areas drivers can turn right at a red light provided they come to a full stop and check to see that the intersection is clear first. The wearing of seat belts is required by law, and you must have a child-protection seats for any passengers under age five.

CONSUMER PROTECTION

Whenever possible, **pay with a major credit card** so you can cancel payment or get reimbursed if there's a problem, provided that you can furnish documentation.

This is the best way to pay, whether you're buying travel arrangements before your trip or shopping at your destination.

If you're doing business with a particular company for the first time, **contact your local Better Business Bureau and the attorney general's offices** in your state and the company's home state, as well. Have any complaints been filed?

Finally, if you're buying a package or tour, always **consider travel insurance** that includes default coverage (☞ Insurance, *below*).

➤ LOCAL BBBs: **Council of Better Business Bureaus** (⌧ 4200 Wilson Blvd., Suite 800, Arlington, VA 22203, ☎ 703/276–0100, FAX 703/525–8277).

CUSTOMS & DUTIES

When shopping, **keep receipts** for all of your purchases. Upon reentering the country **be ready to show customs officials what you've bought.** If you feel a duty is incorrect, appeal the assessment. If you object to the way your clearance was handled, get the inspector's badge number. In either case, first ask to see a supervisor, then write to the appropriate authorities, beginning with the port director at your point of entry.

IN CANADA

Canadian residents who have been out of Canada for at least seven days may bring in C$500 worth of goods duty-free. If you've been away less than seven days but more than 48 hours, the duty-free allowance drops to C$200; if your trip lasts 24–48 hours, the allowance is C$50. You may not pool allowances with family members. Goods claimed under the C$500 exemption may follow you by mail; those claimed under the lesser exemptions must accompany you. Alcohol and tobacco products may be included in the seven-day and 48-hour exemptions but not in the 24-hour exemption. If you meet the age requirements of the province or territory through which you reenter Canada, you may bring in, duty-free, 1.14 liters (40 imperial ounces) of wine or liquor *or* 24 12-ounce cans or bottles of beer or ale. If you are 16 or older, you may bring in, duty-free, 200 cigarettes and 50 cigars.

You may send an unlimited number of gifts worth up to C$60 each duty-free to Canada. Label the package UNSOLICITED GIFT—VALUE UNDER $60. Alcohol and tobacco are excluded.

➤ INFORMATION: **Revenue Canada** (⌧ 2265 St. Laurent Blvd. S, Ottawa, Ontario K1G 4K3, ☎ 613/993–0534, 800/461–9999 in Canada).

IN THE U.K.

From countries outside the European Union, including the United States, you may import, duty-free, 200 cigarettes or 50 cigars; 1 liter of spirits or 2 liters of fortified or sparkling wine or liqueurs; 2 liters of still table wine; 60 milliliters of perfume; 250 milliliters of toilet water; plus £136 worth of other goods, including gifts and souvenirs.

➤ INFORMATION: **HM Customs and Excise** (✉ Dorset House, Stamford St., London SE1 9NG, ☎ 0171/202–4227).

IN THE U.S.
Non-U.S. residents ages 21 and older may import into the United States 200 cigarettes or 50 cigars or 2 kilograms of tobacco, 1 liter of alcohol, and gifts worth $100. Prohibited items include meat products, seeds, plants, and fruits.

➤ INFORMATION: **U.S. Customs Service** (✉ Inquiries, Box 7407, Washington, DC 20044, ☎ 202/927–6724; complaints, Office of Regulations and Rulings, ✉ 1301 Constitution Ave. NW, Washington, DC 20229; registration of equipment, Resource Management, ✉ 1301 Constitution Ave. NW, Washington, DC 20229, ☎ 202/927–0540).

DISABILITIES & ACCESSIBILITY

Most of the region's national parks and recreational areas have accessible visitor centers, rest rooms, campsites, and trails.

➤ LOCAL RESOURCES: **National Park Service, Intermountain Support Office** (✉ Box 728, Santa Fe 87504, ☎ 505/988–6011).

MAKING RESERVATIONS
When discussing accessibility with an operator or reservations agent, **ask hard questions.** Are there any stairs, inside *or* out? Are there grab bars next to the toilet *and* in the shower/tub? How wide is the doorway to the room? To the bathroom? For the most extensive facilities meeting the latest legal specifications, **opt for newer accommodations,** which are more likely to have been designed with access in mind. Older buildings or ships may have more limited facilities. Be sure to **discuss your needs before booking.**

TRANSPORTATION
➤ COMPLAINTS: **Disability Rights Section** (✉ U.S. Department of Justice, Civil Rights Division, Box 66738, Washington, DC 20035–6738, ☎ 202/514–0301 or 800/514–0301, TTY 202/514–0383 or 800/514–0383, FAX 202/307–1198) for general complaints. **Aviation Consumer Protection Division** (☞ Air Travel, *above*) for airline-related problems. **Civil Rights Office** (✉ U.S. Department of Transportation, Departmental Office of Civil Rights, S-30, 400 7th St. SW, Room 10215, Washington, DC, 20590, ☎ 202/366–4648, FAX 202/366–9371) for problems with surface transportation.

DISCOUNTS & DEALS

Be a smart shopper and **compare all your options** before making any choice. A plane ticket bought with a promotional coupon may not be cheaper than the least expensive fare from a discount ticket agency. For high-price travel purchases, such as packages or tours, keep in mind that what you get is just as important as what you save. Because something is cheap doesn't mean it's a bargain.

CLUBS & COUPONS

Many companies sell discounts in the form of travel clubs and coupon books, but these cost money. You must use participating advertisers to get a deal, and only after you recoup the initial membership cost or book price do you begin to save. If you plan to use the club or coupons frequently, you may save considerably. Before signing up, find out what discounts you get for free.

➤ DISCOUNT CLUBS: **Entertainment Travel Editions** (⊠ 2125 Butterfield Rd., Troy, MI 48084, ☎ 800/445–4137; $20–$51, depending on destination). **Great American Traveler** (⊠ Box 27965, Salt Lake City, UT 84127, ☎ 801/974–3033 or 800/548–2812; $49.95 per year). **Moment's Notice Discount Travel Club** (⊠ 7301 New Utrecht Ave., Brooklyn, NY 11204, ☎ 718/234–6295; $25 per year). **Privilege Card International** (⊠ 237 E. Front St., Youngstown, OH 44503, ☎ 330/746–5211 or 800/236–9732; $74.95 per year). **Sears's Mature Outlook** (⊠ Box 9390, Des Moines, IA 50306, ☎ 800/336–6330; $19.95 per year).

Travelers Advantage (⊠ CUC Travel Service, 3033 S. Parker Rd., Suite 1000, Aurora, CO 80014, ☎ 800/548–1116 or 800/648–4037; $59.95 per year). **Worldwide Discount Travel Club** (⊠ 1674 Meridian Ave., Miami Beach, FL 33139, ☎ 305/534–2082; $50 per year family, $40 single).

CREDIT-CARD BENEFITS

When you use your credit card to make travel purchases you may get free travel-accident insurance, collision-damage insurance, and medical or legal assistance, depending on the card and the bank that issued it. American Express, MasterCard, and Visa provide one or more of these services, so **get a copy of your credit card's travel-benefits policy.** If you are a member of an auto club, always **ask hotel and car-rental reservations agents about auto-club discounts.** Some clubs offer additional discounts on tours, cruises, and admission to attractions.

DISCOUNT RESERVATIONS

Look into discount-reservations services with toll-free numbers, which use their buying power to get a better price on hotels, airline tickets, even car rentals. When booking a room always **call the hotel's local toll-free number** (if one is available) rather than the central reservations number—you'll often get a better price. Always ask about special packages or corporate rates.

When shopping for the best deal on hotels and car rentals **look for guaranteed exchange rates,** which protect you against a falling dollar. With your rate locked in you won't pay more, even if the price goes up in the local currency.

➤ AIRLINE TICKETS: ☎ 800/FLY–4–LESS. ☎ 800/FLY–ASAP.

➤ HOTEL ROOMS: **Room Finders USA** (☎ 800/473–7829). **RMC Travel** (☎ 800/245–5738).

PACKAGE DEALS

Packages and guided tours can save you money, but don't confuse the two. When you buy a package, your travel remains independent, just as though you had planned and booked the trip yourself. Fly-drive packages, which combine airfare and car rental, are often a good deal. In cities, ask the local visitor's bureau about hotel packages. These often include tickets to major museum exhibits and other special events.

ETIQUETTE & BEHAVIOR

See Reservations and Pueblos *in* the Pleasures and Pastimes section of Chapter 1 for information about proper etiquette when visiting Native American lands.

GAY & LESBIAN TRAVEL

Although Santa Fe doesn't have a highly visible gay community or a swinging gay nightlife (at press time the city had but one gay bar), lesbians and gay men have long been a presence, and a short sec-

tion of North Guadalupe Street is developing into a local hangout. The monthly *Out! Magazine* (no relation to the national magazine *Out*) provides coverage of New Mexico. A chapter in *Fodor's Gay Guide to the USA* covers Santa Fe, Taos, and Albuquerque. Several travel agencies book tours or make reservations for gay men and lesbians traveling to the state.

➤ RESOURCES: *Fodor's Gay Guide to the USA,* available in bookstores or from Fodor's Travel Publications (☎ 800/533–6478; $20 plus $4 shipping). *Out! Magazine* (☎ 505/243–2540).

HEALTH

MEDICAL PLANS

No one plans to get sick while traveling, but it happens, so **consider signing up with a medical-assistance company.** Members get doctor referrals, emergency evacuation or repatriation, 24-hour telephone hot lines for medical consultation, cash for emergencies, and other personal assistance. Coverage varies by plan, so **review the benefits of each carefully.**

➤ MEDICAL-ASSISTANCE COMPANIES: **International SOS Assistance** (✉ 8 Neshaminy Interplex, Suite 207, Trevose, PA 19053, ☎ 215/245–4707 or 800/523–6586, 📠 215/244–9617; ✉ 12 Chemin Riantbosson, 1217 Meyrin 1, Geneva, Switzerland, ☎ 4122/785–6464, 📠 4122/785–6424; ✉ 10 Anson Rd., 14-07/08

International Plaza, Singapore, 079903, ☎ 65/226–3936, ℻ 65/226–3937).

HOLIDAYS

Major national holidays include New Year's Day; Martin Luther King Jr. Day (third Mon. in Jan.); President's Day (third Mon. in Feb.); Memorial Day (last Mon. in May); Independence Day (July 4); Labor Day (first Mon. in Sept.); Thanksgiving Day (fourth Thurs. in Nov.); Christmas Eve and Day; and New Year's Eve.

INSURANCE

Travel insurance is the best way to **protect yourself against financial loss.** The most useful plan is a comprehensive policy that includes coverage for trip cancellation and interruption, default, trip delay, and medical expenses (with a waiver for preexisting conditions).

Without insurance you will lose all or most of your money if you cancel your trip, regardless of the reason. Default insurance covers you if your tour operator, airline, or cruise line goes out of business. Trip-delay covers unforeseen expenses that you may incur due to bad weather or mechanical delays. It's important to compare the fine print regarding trip-delay coverage when comparing policies.

For overseas travel, one of the most important components of travel insurance is its medical coverage. Supplemental health insurance will pick up the cost of your medical bills should you get sick or injured while traveling. Residents of the United Kingdom can buy an annual travel-insurance policy valid for most vacations taken during the year in which the coverage is purchased. If you are pregnant or have a preexisting condition, make sure you're covered. British citizens should buy extra medical coverage when traveling overseas, according to the Association of British Insurers.

Always **buy travel insurance directly from the insurance company**; if you buy it from a cruise line, airline, or tour operator that goes out of business, you probably will not be covered for the agency or operator's default, a major risk. Before you make any purchase, **review your existing health and home-owner's policies** to find out whether they cover expenses incurred while traveling.

➤ TRAVEL INSURERS: In the U.S., **Access America** (✉ 6600 W. Broad St., Richmond, VA 23230, ☎ 804/285–3300 or 800/284–8300). **Travel Guard International** (✉ 1145 Clark St., Stevens Point, WI 54481, ☎ 715/345–0505 or 800/826–1300). In Canada, **Mutual of Omaha** (✉ Travel Division, 500 University Ave., Toronto, Ontario M5G 1V8, ☎ 416/598–4083, 800/268–8825 in Canada).

➤ INSURANCE INFORMATION: In the U.K., **Association of British Insur-**

ers (✉ 51 Gresham St., London
EC2V 7HQ, ☎ 0171/600–3333).

LODGING

Accommodations in New Mexico
include chain hotels, many bed-
and-breakfasts, small alpine
lodges near the primary ski resorts, and low-budget motels.
Rates are highest during the peak
tourist months of July and August. Off-season rates, which fluctuate, tend to be 20% lower than
peak rates, and reservations are
easier to obtain at this time. You
can book rooms (and rental cars
and outdoor and other activities)
by calling **New Mexico Central
Reservations.**

➤ RESERVATIONS: **New Mexico
Central Reservations** (☎ 800/
466–7829).

B&BS

B&Bs in New Mexico run the
gamut from rooms in locals'
homes to grandly restored adobe
or Victorian homes.

➤ RESERVATION SERVICES: **Bed
and Breakfast of New Mexico**
(☎ 505/982–3332). **New Mexico
Bed and Breakfast Association**
(☎ 505/766–5380 or 800/661–
6649).

HOTELS

Most hotels will hold your reservation until 6 PM; **call ahead if you
plan to arrive late.** Some will hold
a late reservation for you if you
reserve with a credit-card number.

When you call to make a reservation, **ask all the necessary questions up front.** If you are arriving
with a car, ask if the hotel has a
parking lot or covered garage and
whether there is an extra fee for
parking. If you like to eat your
meals in, ask if the hotel has a
restaurant or whether it has room
service (most do, but not necessar-
ily 24 hours a day—and be fore-
warned that it can be expensive).
Most hotels and motels have in-
room TVs, often with cable
movies, but verify this if you like
to watch TV. If you want an in-
room crib for your child, there will
probably be an additional charge.

➤ HOTEL CHAIN TOLL-FREE
NUMBERS: **Best Western** (☎ 800/
528–1234). **Clarion** (☎ 800/
252–7466). **Comfort Inn** (☎ 800/
228–5150). **Days Inn** (☎ 800/
325–2525). **Doubletree and Red
Lion Hotels** (☎ 800/528–0444).
Embassy Suites (☎ 800/362–
2779). **Hilton** (☎ 800/445–
8667). **Holiday Inn** (☎ 800/
465–4329). **Howard Johnson**
(☎ 800/654–4656). **Hyatt Hotels
& Resorts** (☎ 800/233–1234).
**Inter-Continental Hotels &
Resorts** (☎ 800/327–0200).
Marriott (☎ 800/228–9290).
Quality Inn (☎ 800/228–5151).
Radisson (☎ 800/333–3333).
Ramada (☎ 800/228–2828).
Ritz-Carlton (☎ 800/241–3333).
Sheraton (☎ 800/325–3535).
Wyndham Hotels & Resorts
(☎ 800/822–4200).

MOTELS

➤ TOLL-FREE NUMBERS: **Econo Lodge** (☎ 800/553–2666). **Hampton Inn** (☎ 800/426–7866). **La Quinta** (☎ 800/531–5900). **Motel 6** (☎ 800/466–8356). **Rodeway** (☎ 800/228–2000). **Super 8** (☎ 800/848–8888).

MONEY

COSTS

Prices in Santa Fe, especially for a meal, can be as expensive as they are in much larger American cities. A three-course meal in a good restaurant can easily cost $40 per person, not including alcoholic beverages, tax, and tip. There are, of course, less expensive places to eat in the city. Rooms at Santa Fe's fancier hotels begin at about $175, though again there are lower-price options.

CREDIT & DEBIT CARDS

Should you use a credit card or a debit card when traveling? Both have benefits. A credit card allows you to delay payment and gives you certain rights as a consumer (☞ Consumer Protection, *above*). A debit card, also known as a check card, deducts funds directly from your checking account and helps you stay within your budget. When you want to rent a car, though, you may still need an old-fashioned credit card. Although you can always *pay* for your car with a debit card, some agencies will not allow you to *reserve* a car with a debit card.

Otherwise, the two types of plastic are virtually the same. Both will get you cash advances at ATMs worldwide if your card is properly programmed with your personal identification number (PIN).

➤ ATM LOCATIONS: **Cirrus** (☎ 800/424–7787). **Plus** (☎ 800/843–7587).

➤ REPORTING LOST CARDS: To report lost or stolen credit cards, call the following toll-free numbers: **American Express** (☎ 800/327–2177); **Discover Card** (☎ 800/347–2683); **Diners Club** (☎ 800/234–6377); **MasterCard** (☎ 800/307–7309); and **Visa** (☎ 800/847–2911).

EXCHANGING MONEY

For the most favorable rates, **change money through banks.** Although fees charged for ATM transactions may be higher abroad than at home, Cirrus and Plus exchange rates are excellent, because they are based on wholesale rates offered only by major banks. You won't do as well at exchange booths in airports or rail and bus stations, in hotels, in restaurants, or in stores, although you may find their hours more convenient. To avoid lines at airport exchange booths, **get a bit of local currency before you leave home.**

➤ EXCHANGE SERVICES: **Chase Currency to Go** (☎ 800/935–9935; 935–9935 in NY, NJ, and CT). **International Currency Express** (☎ 888/842–0880 on the

East Coast, 888/278–6628 on the West Coast). **Thomas Cook Currency Services** (☎ 800/287–7362 for telephone orders and retail locations).

TRAVELER'S CHECKS

Do you need traveler's checks? It depends on where you're headed. If you're going to rural areas and small towns, go with cash; traveler's checks are best used in cities. Lost or stolen checks can usually be replaced within 24 hours. To ensure a speedy refund, buy your own traveler's checks—don't let someone else pay for them: irregularities like this can cause delays. The person who bought the checks should make the call to request a refund.

OUTDOOR ACTIVITIES & SPORTS

The New Mexico Department of Tourism (☞ Visitor Information, *below*) distributes a booklet, *Outdoors New Mexico,* with information about the many recreational activities that take place within the state.

PACKING

LUGGAGE

How many carry-on bags you can bring with you is up to the airline. Some airlines still allow two, but most (including United, a major carrier in New Mexico) will only let you bring one aboard. Gate agents will take excess baggage—including bags they deem oversize—from you as you board and add it to checked luggage. To avoid this situation, make sure that everything you carry aboard will fit under your seat. Also, get to the gate early, and request a seat at the back of the plane; you'll probably board first, while the overhead bins are still empty. Because big, bulky baggage attracts the attention of gate agents and flight attendants on a busy flight, make sure your carry-on is really a carry-on. Finally, a carry-on that's long and narrow is more likely to remain unnoticed than one that's wide and squarish.

If you are flying internationally, note that baggage allowances may be determined not by piece but by weight—generally 88 pounds (40 kilograms) in first class, 66 pounds (30 kilograms) in business class, and 44 pounds (20 kilograms) in economy.

Airline liability for baggage is limited to $1,250 per person on flights within the United States. On international flights it amounts to $9.07 per pound or $20 per kilogram for checked baggage (roughly $640 per 70-pound bag) and $400 per passenger for unchecked baggage. You can buy additional coverage at check-in for about $10 per $1,000 of coverage, but it excludes a rather extensive list of items, shown on your airline ticket.

Before departure, **itemize your bags' contents** and their worth, and label the bags with your name, address, and phone number.

(If you use your home address, cover it so that potential thieves can't see it readily.) **Pack a copy of your itinerary** inside each bag. At check-in, **make sure that each bag is correctly tagged** with the destination airport's three-letter code. If your bags arrive damaged or fail to arrive at all, file a written report with the airline before leaving the airport.

PACKING LIST

Typical of the Southwest, temperatures can vary considerably from sunup to sundown. You should **pack for warm days and chilly nights.**

New Mexico is one of the most informal and laid-back areas of the country, which for many is much a part of its appeal. Probably no more than three or four restaurants in the entire state enforce a dress code, even for dinner, though men are likely to feel more comfortable wearing a jacket in the major hotel dining rooms, and anyone wearing tennis shoes may receive a look of stern disapproval from the maître d'.

The Western look, popular throughout the country a few years back, has, of course, never lost its hold on the West. But Western dress has become less corny and more subtle and refined. Western-style clothes are no longer a costume; they're being mixed with tweed jackets, for example, for a more conservative, sophisticated image. Which is to say, you can dress Western with your boots and big belt buckles in even the best places in Santa Fe and Taos, but if you come strolling through the lobby of the Eldorado Hotel looking like Hopalong Cassidy, you'll get some funny looks.

PASSPORTS & VISAS

When traveling internationally **carry a passport even if you don't need one** (it's always the best form of ID), and make **two photocopies of the data page** (one for someone at home and another for you, carried separately from your passport). If you lose your passport, promptly call the nearest embassy or consulate and the local police.

VISA OFFICES

➤ U.K. CITIZENS: **U.S. Embassy Visa Information Line** (☎ 01891/ 200290; calls cost 49p per minute, 39p per minute cheap rate), for U.S. visa information. **U.S. Embassy Visa Branch** (✉ 5 Upper Grosvenor St., London W1A 2JB), for U.S. visa information; send a self-addressed, stamped envelope. Write the **U.S. Consul General** (✉ Queen's House, Queen St., Belfast BTI 6EO) if you live in Northern Ireland.

PASSPORT OFFICES

The best time to apply for a passport or to renew is during the fall and winter. Before any trip, be sure to check your passport's expiration date and, if necessary, renew it as soon as possible. (Some countries won't allow you to enter on a passport that's due to expire in six months or less.)

➤ U.K. CITIZENS: **London Passport Office** (☎ 0990/21010), to find out fees and documentation requirements and to request an emergency passport.

TELEPHONES

COUNTRY CODES

The country code for the United States and Canada is 1.

DIRECTORY & OPERATOR INFORMATION

For assistance from an operator, dial "0." To find out a telephone number in New Mexico (or anywhere in the United States), call US West directory assistance, 1 + 411. If you want to charge a long-distance call to the person you're calling, you can call collect by dialing "0" instead of "1" before the 10-digit number, and an operator will come on the line to assist you (the party you're calling, however, has the right to refuse the call).

INTERNATIONAL CALLS

Calls to destinations outside the U.S. and Canada can be direct-dialed from most phones; dial "011," followed by the country code and then the local number (the front pages of many local telephone directories include a list of overseas country codes). To have an operator assist you, dial

"0" and ask for the overseas operator. The country code for the United Kingdom is 44.

LONG-DISTANCE CALLS

Competitive long-distance carriers make calling within the United States relatively convenient and let you avoid hotel surcharges. By dialing an 800 number, you can get connected to the long-distance company of your choice.

➤ LONG-DISTANCE CARRIERS: **AT&T** (☎ 800/225–5288). **MCI** (☎ 800/888–8000). **Sprint** (☎ 800/366–2255).

PUBLIC PHONES

Local calls from pay telephones in New Mexico cost 35¢.

TRAIN TRAVEL

Amtrak trains stop in Lamy, south of Santa Fe.

➤ TRAIN SCHEDULES: **Amtrak** (☎ 800/872–7245).

TRAVEL AGENCIES

A good travel agent puts your needs first. Look for an agency that has been in business at least five years, emphasizes customer service, and has someone on staff who specializes in your destination. In addition, **make sure the agency belongs to a professional trade organization,** such as ASTA in the United States.

➤ LOCAL AGENT REFERRALS: **American Society of Travel Agents** (ASTA, ☎ 800/965–2782 for 24-

hr hot line, FAX 703/684–8319). **Association of Canadian Travel Agents** (⊠ Suite 201, 1729 Bank St., Ottawa, Ontario K1V 7Z5, ☎ 613/521–0474, FAX 613/521–0805). **Association of British Travel Agents** (⊠ 55–57 Newman St., London W1P 4AH, ☎ 0171/637–2444, FAX 0171/637–0713).

VISITOR INFORMATION

For general information before you go, contact the city and state tourism bureaus. If you're interested in learning more about the area's national forests, contact the U.S. Forest Service. And, for information about Native American attractions, call or visit the Indian Pueblo Cultural Center.

➤ CITY INFORMATION: *See* Santa Fe A to Z in Chapter 2 *and* Taos A to Z *in* Chapter 3.

➤ STATEWIDE INFORMATION: **New Mexico Department of Tourism** (⊠ 491 Old Santa Fe Trail, Santa Fe 87503, ☎ 505/827–7400 or 800/545–2070, FAX 505/827–7402).

➤ NATIONAL FORESTS: **U.S. Forest Service, Southwestern Region** (⊠ Public Affairs Office, 517 Gold Ave. SW, Albuquerque 87102, ☎ 505/842–3292, FAX 505/842–3800).

➤ NATIVE ATTRACTIONS: **Indian Pueblo Cultural Center** (⊠ 2401 12th St. NW, Albuquerque 87102, ☎ 505/843–7270 or 800/766–4405 outside NM, FAX 505/842–6959.)

➤ IN THE U.K.: **New Mexico Tourism Bureau** (⊠ 302 Garden Studios, 11–15 Betterton St., Covent Garden, London WC2H 9BP, ☎ 0171/470–8803, FAX 0171/470–8810).

U.S. GOVERNMENT

Government agencies can be an excellent source of inexpensive travel information. When planning your trip, **find out what government materials are available.**

➤ PAMPHLETS: **Consumer Information Center** (⊠ Consumer Information Catalogue, Pueblo, CO 81009, ☎ 719/948–3334 or 888/878–3256) for a free catalog that includes travel titles.

WEB SITES

The official Web sites of, respectively, the state of New Mexico, Santa Fe, and Taos are as follows: **www.newmexico.org**, **www.santafe.org**, and **taoswebb.com/taos**. For maps, visit the **gonewmexico.miningco.com** site, which has links to sites of campgrounds, municipalities, and commercial businesses.

WHEN TO GO

The majority of major events—including the Santa Fe Opera, Chamber Music Festival, and Indian and Spanish markets—are geared to the traditionally heavy tourist season of July and August. The Santa Fe Fiesta is held in September.

The relatively cool climates of Santa Fe and Taos are a lure in summer, as is the skiing in Taos and Santa Fe in winter. Hotel rates are generally highest during the peak summer season but fluctuate less than those in most major resort areas. If you plan to come in summer, **be sure to make reservations in advance for July and August.** You can avoid most of the tourist crowds by coming during spring or fall. Spring weather is unpredictable; sudden storms may erupt. October is one of the best months to visit: The air is crisp, colors are brilliant, and whole mountainsides become fluttering cascades of red and gold.

➤ FORECASTS: **Weather Channel Connection** (☎ 900/932–8437), 95¢ per minute from a Touch-Tone phone.

CLIMATE

The following are average daily maximum and minimum temperatures for Santa Fe.

Jan.	39F	4C	May	68F	20C	Sept.	73F	23C
	19	–7		42	6		48	9
Feb.	42F	6C	June	78F	26C	Oct.	62F	17C
	23	–5		51	11		37	3
Mar.	51F	11C	July	80F	27C	Nov.	50F	10C
	28	–2		57	14		28	–2
Apr.	59F	15C	Aug.	78F	26C	Dec.	39F	4C
	35	2		55	13		19	–7

1 Destination: Santa Fe and Taos

CITIES OF ENCHANTMENT

NEW MEXICO'S tagline is more than a marketing cliché. The state is truly a "Land of Enchantment," and Santa Fe is indisputably "the City Different." Surrounded by mind-expanding mountain views and filled with sinuous streets that discourage car traffic but invite leisurely exploration, Santa Fe welcomes with characteristic warmth, if not some trepidation. Rapid growth and development have taken their toll, prompting many local residents to worry about becoming too much like "everywhere else," and you'll hear various complaints about encroaching commercialism and its attendant T-shirt shops and fast-food restaurants that interfere with the rhythms of life here.

But despite (or perhaps, occasionally, because of) a surfeit of trendy restaurants, galleries, and boutiques that tout regional fare and wares, both authentic and artificial, Santa Fe remains a special place to visit. Commercialism notwithstanding, its deeply spiritual aura affects even nonreligious types in surprising ways, inspiring a reverence probably not unlike that which inspired the Spanish monks to name it the "City of Holy Faith." (Its full name is La Villa Real de la Santa Fe de San Francisco de Asís, or the Royal City of the Holy Faith of St. Francis of Assisi.) A kind of mystical Catholicism blended with ancient Native American lore and beliefs flourishes throughout northern New Mexico in tiny mountain villages that have seen little change through the centuries. Tales of miracles, spontaneous healings, and spiritual visitations thrive in the old adobe churches that line the High Road that leads north of Santa Fe to Taos.

If Santa Fe is spiritual, sophisticated, and occasionally superficial, Taos, 65 mi away, is very much an outpost despite its relative proximity to the capital. Compared with Santa Fe, Taos is smaller, feistier, quirkier, tougher, and very independent. Taoseños are a study in contradictions: Wary of strangers and suspicious of outsiders, they nevertheless accept visitors with genuine warmth and pride. Rustic and delightfully unpretentious, the town contains a handful of upscale restaurants with cuisines and wine lists as innovative as what you might find in New York. It's a haven for aging hippies, creative geniuses, cranky misanthropes, and anyone else who wants a good quality of life in a place that accepts new arrivals without a lot of questions—as long as they don't offend longtime residents with their city attitudes.

Unifying these towns and the terrain around them is the appeal of the land and the people. It's the character of the residents and their attitude toward the land that imbue New Mexico with its enchanted spirit. First-time visitors discover the unexpected pleasures of a place where time is measured not by linear calculations of hours, days, weeks, and years but in a circular sweep of crop cycles, gestation periods, the rotation of generations, and the changing of seasons.

— Nancy Zimmerman

WHAT'S WHERE

Santa Fe

On a 7,000-ft-high plateau at the base of the Sangre de Cristo Mountains in north-central New Mexico, Santa Fe is one of the most popular cities in the United States, with an abundance of museums, one-of-a-kind cultural events, art galleries, first-rate restaurants, and shops selling Southwestern furnishings and cowboy gear. Among the smallest state capitals in the country, the city is characterized by its Pueblo Revival–style homes and buildings made of adobe. The remnants of a 2,000-year-old Pueblo civilization surround the city, and this also echoes its nearly 250 years of Spanish and Mexican rule.

Taos

About 65 mi north of Santa Fe, on a rolling mesa at the base of the Sangre de Cristo Mountains, Taos is a world-famous artistic and literary center that attracts artists and collectors to its museums and galleries. Romantic courtyards, stately elms and cottonwood trees, narrow streets, and a profusion of adobe buildings are but a few of the charms of this city of 6,500 people. Three miles northwest of the commercial center lies Taos Pueblo, and south of town is Ranchos de Taos, a farming and ranching community first settled centuries ago by the Spanish.

NEW AND NOTEWORTHY

The massive remodeling of the facility of the **Santa Fe Opera** was completed in time for the 1998 summer season opening. The major change is the addition of a covering of masts and rods, similar to a suspension bridge, to provide shelter over the outdoor seating.

Several high-end Santa Fe restaurants have become more affordable with the introduction of prix-fixe menus, early-bird dinners, and one-price-entrée nights. Check on the availability of these specials when making reservations; you might save a bundle.

In **Taos** the dining scene has never been better. The success of several restaurants during the past few years, among them the Trading Post, Joseph's Table, La Folie, and Fred's Place, has inspired some of the older establishments to update their menus. The result is more variety, higher quality, and a choice of ambience.

PLEASURES AND PASTIMES

Dining

New Mexico's cuisine is a delicious and extraordinary mixture of Pueblo, Spanish colonial, and Mexican and American frontier cooking. Recipes that came from Spain via Mexico were adapted for local ingredients—chiles, corn, pork, wild game, pinto beans, honey, apples, and piñon nuts—and have remained much the same ever since.

In Santa Fe and Taos, babies cut their teeth on **fresh flour tortillas** and quickly develop a taste for **sopaipillas,** deep-fried, puff-pastry pillows, drizzled with honey. But it is the **chile pepper,** whether red or green, that is the heart and soul of northern New Mexican cuisine. You might be a bit surprised to learn that *ristras,* those strings of bright red chiles that seem to hang everywhere, are sold more

for eating here than for decoration. More varieties of chiles —upward of 90—are grown in New Mexico than anywhere else in the world. *See* the Glossary at the back of this book for names and terms of traditional New Mexican dishes.

In most restaurants you can dress as casually as you like. Those in the major business hotels tend to be a bit more formal, but as the evening wears down, so do the restrictions.

Outdoor Activities and Sports

CANOEING AND RAFTING➤ You can challenge yourself on New Mexico's rivers. The **Taos Box,** a 17-mi run through the churning rapids of the Rio Grande, is one of America's most exciting rafting experiences.

GOLF➤ With several dozen courses, the state has a respectable share of turf, and the dry climate makes playing very comfortable. There are excellent public courses in Santa Fe and Taos.

HORSE RACING➤ Horse racing with pari-mutuel betting is very popular in New Mexico. One of the more favored of the state's tracks is **Downs at Santa Fe,** 5 mi south of town.

SKIING➤ New Mexico contains many world-class downhill ski areas. Snowmaking equipment is used in most areas to ensure a long season, usually from Thanksgiving through Easter. The **Santa Fe Ski Area** averages 250 inches of dry-powder snow a year; it accommodates all levels of skiers on more than 40 trails. Within a 90-mi radius of Taos are resorts with slopes for all levels of skiers, as well as snowmobile and cross-country ski trails. The **Taos Ski Valley** resort is recognized internationally for its challenging terrain and European-style ambience.

Parks and Monuments

New Mexico's state-park network includes nearly four dozen parks, ranging from high-mountain lakes and pine forests in the north to the Chihuahuan Desert lowlands of the south. Parks and monuments close to Santa Fe include **Pecos National Historic Park and Jemez State Monument.** The **Carson National Forest** is near Taos.

Reservations and Pueblos

New Mexico's Pueblo cultures, each with its own reservation, and distinct but overlapping history, art, and customs, evolved out of the highly civilized Anasazi culture that built Chaco Canyon. Pueblos dating back centuries are located near Santa Fe and Taos; the best time to visit them is during one of their many year-round public dance ceremonies. Admission is free to pueblos unless otherwise indicated. Donations, however, are always welcome.

The pueblos around Santa Fe— San Ildefonso, Nambé, Pojoaque, and Santa Clara—are more infused with Spanish culture than are the pueblos in other areas. Dwellers here also have the keenest business sense when dealing with the sale of handicrafts and art and with matters touristic. The famous Taos Pueblo, unchanged through the centuries, is the personification of classic Pueblo Native American culture. It and the Picurís Pueblo near Taos have first-rate recreational facilities. For detailed information about the individual pueblos, *see* Chapters 2 and 3.

When visiting pueblos and reservations, you're expected to follow a certain etiquette. Each pueblo has its own regulations for the use of still and video cameras and video and tape recorders, as well as for sketching and painting. Some pueblos prohibit photography altogether. Others, such as Santa Clara, prohibit photography at certain times, such as during ritual dances. Still others allow photography but require a permit, which usually costs about $5 or $10 for a still camera. The privilege of setting up an easel and painting all day will cost you as little as $35 or as much as $150 (at Taos Pueblo). Be sure to ask permission before photographing anyone in the pueblos; it's also customary to give the subject a dollar or two for agreeing to be photographed. Native American law prevails on the pueblos, and violations of photography regulations could result in confiscation of cameras.

Specific restrictions for the various pueblos are noted in the individual descriptions. Other rules are described below.

- Possessing or using drugs and/or alcohol on Native American land is forbidden.

- Ritual dances often have serious religious significance and should be respected as such. Silence is mandatory—that means no questions about ceremonies or dances while they're being performed. Don't walk across the dance plaza during a performance, and don't applaud afterward.

- Kiva and ceremonial rooms are restricted to pueblo members.

- Cemeteries are sacred. They're off-limits to all visitors and should never be photographed.

- Unless pueblo dwellings are clearly marked as shops, don't wander or peek inside. Remember, these are private homes.

- Many of the pueblo buildings are hundreds of years old. Don't try to scale adobe walls or climb on top of buildings, or you may come tumbling down.

- Don't litter. Nature is sacred on the pueblos, and defacing land can be a serious offense.

Shopping

ANTIQUES➤ You'll find everything in New Mexico's shops, from early Mexican typewriters to period saddles, ceramic pots, farm tools, pioneer aviation equipment, and yellowed newspaper clippings about Kit Carson and D. H. Lawrence.

ART➤ Santa Fe, with more than 150 galleries, is the arts capital of the Southwest and a leading arts center nationally. Taos is not far behind. Native American art, Western art, Hispanic art, contemporary art, sculpture, photography, prints, ceramics, jewelry, folk art, junk art—it's all for sale in New Mexico, produced by artists of international and local renown.

CRAFTS➤ Hispanic handcrafted furniture and *santos* (saints) command high prices from collectors. Santos are religious carvings and paintings in the form of *bultos* (three-dimensional carvings) and *retablos* (holy images painted on wood or tin). Colorful handwoven Hispanic textiles, tinwork, ironwork, and straw appliqué are also in demand. Native American textiles, rugs, kachina dolls, baskets, silver jewelry, turquoise, pottery, beadwork, ornamental shields, drums, and ceramics can be found almost everywhere. Prices range from thousands of dollars for a rare 1930s kachina doll to a few cents for hand-wrapped bundles of sage, juniper, sweet grass, and lavender that are used by Native Americans in healing ceremonies, gatherings, and daily cleansing of the home.

SPICES➤ Roadside stands sell chile ristras, and shops all over the state carry chile powder and other spices. You'll catch the smell of chile peppers from the road; walk in a store and your eyes may water and your mouth salivate. For many, especially natives of the Southwest, *picante* is the purest, finest word in the Spanish language. It means hot—spicy hot. All around you, in boxes, bags, packets, jars, and cans, there's everything picante—salsas, chile pastes, powders, herbs, spices, peppers, barbecue sauce, and fiery potions in bottles.

FODOR'S CHOICE

Historic Buildings

★ **Palace of the Governors, Santa Fe.** This Pueblo-style structure has served as the residence for 100 Spanish, Native American, Mexican, and American governors; it is now the state history museum.

★ **San Francisco de Asís Church, Ranchos de Taos.** Built in the 18th century as a spiritual and physical refuge from raiding Apaches, Utes, and Comanches, this church is a spectacular example of adobe Mission architecture.

★ **San Miguel Mission, Santa Fe.** The oldest church still in use in the continental United States, this simple, earth-hued adobe structure built in about 1625 has priceless statues and paintings on display.

★ **Taos Pueblo, Taos.** For nearly 1,000 years the Taos-Tiwas have lived at or near this site, the largest existing multistory pueblo structure in the United States.

Lodging

★ **Inn of the Anasazi, Santa Fe.** This decidedly upscale hotel has individually designed rooms, each with a beamed ceiling, kiva fireplace, four-poster bed, and handcrafted desk, dresser, and tables. *$$$$*

★ **The Bavarian, Taos.** A luxurious secluded hideaway, this authentic re-creation of a Bavarian ski lodge has the only mid-mountain accommodations in the Taos Ski Valley. *$$$*

★ **Touchstone Inn, Taos.** This peaceful bed-and-breakfast overlooking the Taos Pueblo is filled with a tasteful mix of antiques and modern artworks by the talented owner, Ben Price. *$$$*

★ **Hacienda del Sol, Taos.** Once a house for guests of art patron Mabel Dodge Luhan, this bed-and-breakfast contains kiva-style fireplaces, Spanish antiques, Southwestern-style handcrafted furniture, and original artworks. *$$–$$$*

Restaurants

★ **Anasazi, Santa Fe.** New Mexican and Native American flavors combine harmoniously in the exotic fare served at Anasazi. *$$$$*

★ **Geronimo, Santa Fe.** The menu changes daily at this popular restaurant in the historic Borrego House. *$$$$*

★ **Trading Post Cafe, Taos.** Imaginative variations on Continental and other dishes have made this relative newcomer a town favorite. *$$$–$$$$*

★ **Casa Fresen Bakery, Taos.** Perfectly packed picnic baskets are a specialty at this espresso bar, bakery, and Italian deli; its gorgeous breads, meats, and cheeses would even make a New Yorker smile. *$$*

★ **Plaza Café, Santa Fe.** A fixture on the Plaza since 1918, this busy restaurant serves excellent American, New Mexican, and Greek fare. *$$*

Romantic Sites

★ **Millicent Rogers Museum, Taos.** At this Native American and Hispanic art museum, the courtyard provides an enchanted atmosphere.

★ **Outdoor hot tubs at Ten Thousand Waves, Santa Fe.** Come to this Japanese-style health spa to unwind after a day's cavorting on the slopes or in the dusty desert.

★ **Santa Fe at Christmastime.** New Mexico's capital is at its most festive at the end of December, with incense and piñon smoke sweetening the air and the winter darkness illuminated by thousands of *farolitos* (tiny candle lanterns in paper sacks).

★ **Santa Fe Opera.** It's hard to surpass the excitement of the curtain rising and the music swelling at an SFO world premier as lightning crackles over the distant Jemez Mountains.

Scenic Drives

★ **Enchanted Circle.** This 84-mi loop from Taos winds through alpine country, with a few colorful mining towns along the way.

★ **High Road to Taos.** On the old road linking Santa Fe and Taos, the stunning drive encompasses rolling hillsides studded with orchards and tiny picturesque villages noted for weavers and wood-carvers.

2 Santa Fe

Updated
by Nancy
Zimmerman

WITH ITS CRISP, CLEAR AIR and bright, sunny weather, Santa Fe couldn't be more welcoming. On a plateau at the base of the Sangre de Cristo Mountains—at an elevation of 7,000 ft—the city is surrounded by remnants of a 2,000-year-old Pueblo civilization and filled with reminders of almost four centuries of Spanish and Mexican rule. The town's placid central Plaza, which dates from the early 17th century, has been the site of bullfights, public floggings, gunfights, battles, political rallies, promenades, and public markets over the years. A uniquely appealing destination, Santa Fe is fabled for its rows of chic art galleries, superb restaurants, and shops selling Southwestern furnishings and cowboy gear.

La Villa Real de la Santa Fe de San Francisco de Asís (the Royal City of the Holy Faith of St. Francis of Assisi) was founded in the early 1600s by Don Pedro de Peralta, who planted his banner in the name of Spain. In 1680 the region's Pueblo people rose in revolt, burning homes and churches and killing hundreds of Spaniards. After an extended siege in Santa Fe, the Spanish colonists were driven out of New Mexico. The tide turned 12 years later, when General Don Diego de Vargas returned with a new army from El Paso and recaptured Santa Fe.

To commemorate de Vargas's victory, Las Fiestas de Santa Fe have been held every year since 1712. The nation's oldest community celebration takes place on the weekend after Labor Day, with parades, mariachis, pageants, and nonstop parties. Though the best-known festival in Santa Fe, "Fiesta" (as it's referred to locally) is but one of many annual opportunities for revelry—from the arrival of the rodeo and the opening week of the Santa Fe Opera in summer to traditional Pueblo dances at Christmastime.

Following de Vargas's defeat of the Pueblos, the once-grand *El Camino Real* (the Royal Road), stretching from Mexico City to Santa Fe, brought an army of conquistadors, clergymen, and settlers to the northernmost reaches of Spain's New World conquests. In 1820 the first flood of covered wagons rolled into the Plaza from Missouri along the Santa Fe Trail—a prime artery of U.S. westward expansion—and a booming trade with the United States was born. After Mexico achieved independence from Spain in 1821, its subsequent rule of New Mexico further increased this exchange.

The Santa Fe Trail's heyday ended with the arrival of the Atchison, Topeka & Santa Fe Railway in 1880. The trains and later the nation's first highways brought a new type of settler to Santa Fe—artists who fell in love with its cultural diversity, history, and magical color and light. Their presence attracted tourists, who quickly became a primary source of income for the largely poor populace.

Santa Fe is renowned for its arts, tricultural (Native American, Hispanic, and Anglo) heritage, and adobe architecture. The Pueblo people were already using adobe—though in a slightly different form—to build their multistory "condos" when the Spanish arrived. In a relatively dry, treeless region, adobe was a naturally suitable building material. Melding into the landscape with their earthen colors and rounded, flowing lines, the pueblos and villages were hard to see from afar and thus somewhat camouflaged from raiding nomadic tribes. The region's distinctive architecture no longer repels visitors, it attracts them.

Among the smallest state capitals in the country, Santa Fe has no major airport (Albuquerque's is the nearest). The city's population, an estimated 62,000, swells to nearly double that figure in summer. In winter the skiers arrive, lured by the challenging slopes of the Santa Fe Ski Area and nearby Taos Ski Valley. Geared for tourists, Santa Fe can put a serious dent in your travel budget. Prices are highest in June, July, and August. Between September and November and in April they're lower, and (except for the major holidays) from December to March they're the lowest.

EXPLORING SANTA FE

Humorist Will Rogers said on his first visit to Santa Fe, "Whoever designed this town did so while riding on a jackass, backwards, and drunk." The maze of narrow streets and alleyways sometimes confounds motorists, but with shops and restaurants, a flowered courtyard, or an eye-catching gallery at nearly every turn they're a delight for pedestrians.

Numbers in the text correspond to numbers in the margin and on the Exploring Santa Fe map.

Santa Fe Plaza

Much of the history of Santa Fe, New Mexico, the South-west, and even the West has roots in Santa Fe's central Plaza, which New Mexico governor Don Pedro de Peralta laid out in 1607. The Plaza, already well established by the time the revolt of the Pueblos occurred in 1680, was the site of a bullring and of fiestas and fandangos. Freight wagons unloaded here after completing their arduous journeys along the Santa Fe Trail. The American flag was raised over the Plaza in 1846 during the Mexican War, which resulted in Mexico losing all its territories in the present southwestern United States. For a time the Plaza was a tree-shaded park with a white picket fence. In the 1890s it was an expanse of lawn where uniformed bands played in an ornate gazebo.

A Good Walk

You can get an overview of the history of Santa Fe and New Mexico at the **Palace of the Governors** ①, which borders the northern side of the Plaza on Palace Avenue. Outside, under the Palace portals, dozens of Native American craftspeople sell their wares. From the Palace, cross Lincoln Street to the **Museum of Fine Arts** ②, where the works of regional masters are on display. The **Georgia O'Keeffe Museum** ③, on nearby Johnson Street, exhibits the works of its namesake, New Mexico's best-known painter.

From the O'Keeffe museum, return to the Plaza and stroll over to its southeastern corner on Old Santa Fe Trail, where you can find the town's oldest hotel, **La Fonda** ④, a good place to soak up a little of bygone Santa Fe. When you leave La Fonda you can't miss the imposing facade of **Saint Francis Cathedral** ⑤, looming above East San Francisco Street. Cross Cathedral Place, away from the church, to get to the **Museum of the Institute of American Indian Arts** ⑥. A stone's throw away from the museum is cool, quiet **Sena Plaza** ⑦.

TIMING

It's possible to zoom through this compact area in about five hours—two hours exploring the Plaza and the Palace of the Governors, two hours seeing the Museum of Fine Arts and the Museum of the Institute of American Indian Arts, and an hour visiting the other sites. Particularly festive times on the Plaza are the weekend after Labor Day, during Las Fiestas de Santa Fe, and at Christmas, when all the trees are filled with lights and lanterns line the rooftops.

Sights to See

❸ Georgia O'Keeffe Museum. One of many East Coast artists who visited New Mexico in the first half of the 20th century, O'Keeffe fell in love with the region and returned to live and paint here, eventually emerging as the demigoddess of Southwestern art. This private museum devoted to her opened in 1997. Its founders hope the facility will eventually exhibit the largest collection of O'Keeffe's works. ⊠ *217 Johnson St.,* ☎ *505/995–0785.* ⊡ *$5, 4-day pass $10 (good at all 4 state museums in Santa Fe), free Fri.* ☉ *Tues.–Thurs. and weekends 10–5, Fri. 10–8.*

❹ La Fonda. A Santa Fe landmark, La Fonda (☞ Lodging, *below*) faces the southeast corner of the Plaza. A *fonda* (inn) has stood on this site for centuries; this hotel was built in 1922. It is referred to as "the Inn at the End of the Trail" because of its proximity to the Plaza and history as a gathering place for cowboys, trappers, traders, soldiers, and frontier politicians. Major social events still take place here. ⊠ *E. San Francisco St. at Old Santa Fe Trail,* ☎ *505/982–5511.*

★ ❷ Museum of Fine Arts. The understated 1917 building that contains one of America's finest regional art museums was Santa Fe's first Pueblo Revival structure. The inspiration for the region's distinctive architectural look, it has ceilings made of split cedar *latillas* (branches set in a crosshatch pattern) and hand-hewn vigas. The 8,000-piece permanent collection emphasizes the works of regional artists, including Georgia O'Keeffe; the "Cinco Pintores" (five painters) of Santa Fe (including Fremont Elis and Will Shuster); members of the Taos Society of Artists (Ernest L. Blumenschein, Bert Geer Philips, Joseph Henry Sharp, and Eanger Irving Couse, among others); as well as works by Mexican, Southwestern, and Native American artists. Many excellent ex-

14

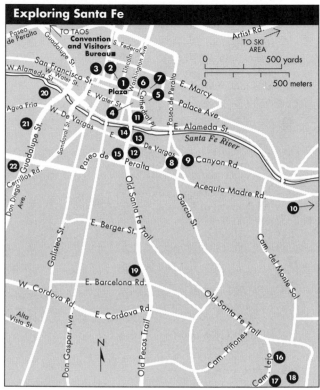

Exploring Santa Fe

Barrio de
Analco, **14**

Canyon Road, **9**

Cristo Rey
Church, **10**

Georgia O'Keeffe
Museum, **3**

Gerald Peters
Gallery, **8**

La Fonda, **4**

Loretto Chapel, **11**

Museum of
Fine Arts, **2**

Museum of
Indian Arts and
Culture, **16**

Museum of the
Institute of
American Indian
Arts, **6**

Museum of
International
Folk Art, **17**

New Mexico
State Capitol, **15**

The Oldest
House, **13**

Palace of the
Governors, **1**

Saint Francis
Cathedral, **5**

San Miguel
Mission, **12**

Santa Fe Children's
Museum, **19**

Santa Fe
Southern
Railway, **21**

Santuario de
Guadalupe, **20**

Sena Plaza, **7**

SITE Santa Fe, **22**

Wheelwright
Museum of the
American
Indian, **18**

amples of Spanish colonial–style furniture are on display. An interior *placita* (small plaza) with fountains, murals, and sculpture, and the breathtaking St. Francis Auditorium are other highlights. Concerts and lectures are often held in the auditorium. ⊠ *W. Palace Ave.,* ☎ *505/827–4455.* ⌸ *$5, 4-day pass $10 (good at the Georgia O'Keeffe Museum and all 4 state museums in Santa Fe), free Fri.* ☉ *Tues.–Thurs. and weekends 10–5, Fri. 10–8.*

❻   **Museum of the Institute of American Indian Arts.** Inside the handsomely renovated former post office, this museum contains the largest collection of contemporary Native American art in the United States. The paintings, photography, sculptures, prints, and traditional crafts exhibited here were created by past and present students and teachers of the seminal Institute of American Indian Arts. The institute, across town on Cerrillos Road, was founded as a one-room studio classroom in the early 1930s by Dorothy Dunn, a beloved art teacher who played a critical role in launching the careers of many Native American artists. In the 1960s and 1970s the institute blossomed into the nation's premier center for Native American arts. Artist Fritz Scholder taught here for years, as did the sculptor Allan Houser. Among their disciples was the painter T. C. Cannon. ⊠ *108 Cathedral Pl.,* ☎ *505/988–6211 for events and parking information.* ⌸ *$4.* ☉ *Mon.–Sat. 10–5, Sun. noon–5.*

★ ☾ ❶   **Palace of the Governors.** A humble-looking one-story adobe on the north side of the Plaza, the palace is the oldest public building in the United States. Built at the same time as the Plaza, circa 1607, the palace was the seat of four regional governments—those of Spain, Mexico, the Confederacy, and the U.S. territory that preceded New Mexico's statehood, which was achieved in 1912. It served as the residence for 100 Spanish, Mexican, and American governors, including Governor Lew Wallace, who wrote his epic *Ben Hur* in its then drafty rooms, all the while complaining of the dust and mud that fell from its earthen ceiling.

The Palace of the Governors, which has been the central headquarters of the Museum of New Mexico since 1913, houses the primary unit of the **State History Museum.** Permanent exhibits chronicle 450 years of New Mexico history using maps, furniture, clothing, housewares, weaponry, and village models. With advance permission, students and researchers have access to the museum's extensive research library and its rare maps, manuscripts, and photographs (more than 120,000 prints and negatives). The palace is also home to the **Museum of New Mexico Press,** which prints books, pamphlets, and cards on antique presses and hosts book-binding demonstrations, lectures, and slide shows. There is also an outstanding gift shop and bookstore. ⊠ *Palace Ave. (north side of the Plaza),* ☎ *505/827–6483.* ☞ *$5, 4-day pass $10 (good at all 4 state museums in Santa Fe and the Georgia O'Keeffe Museum), free Fri.* ⊙ *Tues.–Sun. 10–5.*

Dozens of **Native American vendors** gather daily under the portal of the Palace of the Governors to display and sell pottery, jewelry, bread, and other goods. With few excep-tions, the more than 500 artists and craftspeople regis-tered to sell under the portals are Pueblo or Navajo Indians. The merchandise for sale here is required to meet Museum of New Mexico standards: All items are handmade or hand-strung in Native American households; silver jewelry is either sterling (92.5% pure) or coin silver (90% pure); all metal jewelry bears the maker's mark, which is regis-tered with the museum. Prices tend to reflect the high qual-ity of the merchandise. Photographs should not be taken without permission.

★ ❺ **Saint Francis Cathedral.** This magnificent cathedral, a block east of the Plaza, is one of the rare significant departures from the city's ubiquitous pueblo architecture. Construc-tion was begun in 1869 by Jean Baptiste Lamy, Santa Fe's first archbishop, working with French architects and Ital-ian stonemasons. The inspiration for Willa Cather's novel *Death Comes for the Archbishop,* Lamy, the circuit-riding cleric who was sent by the Catholic Church to the South-west to change the religious practices of its native popula-tion (to "civilize" them, as one period document puts it), is buried in the crypt beneath the church's high altar.

A small adobe chapel on the northeastern side of the cathe-dral, the remnant of an earlier church built on the site, em-bodies the Hispanic architectural influence so conspicuously absent from the Romanesque cathedral itself. The chapel's *Nuestra Señora de la Paz* (Our Lady of Peace), the oldest Madonna statue in the United States, accompanied Don

Diego de Vargas on his reconquest of Santa Fe in 1692, a feat attributed to the statue's spiritual intervention. Every Friday the faithful adorn the statue with a new dress. ⊠ *231 Cathedral Pl.,* ☎ *505/982–5619.* ☉ *Mass celebrated Mon.–Sat. at 7 and 8:15 AM, 12:10 and 5:15 PM; Sun. at 6, 8, and 10 AM, noon, and 7 PM.*

❼ Sena Plaza. Two-story buildings surround this courtyard, which can be entered only through two small doorways on Palace Avenue. Flowering fruit trees, a fountain, and inviting benches provide a quiet setting that harks back to a simpler time. The buildings, erected in the 1700s as a single-family residence, had quarters for blacksmiths, bakers, farmers, and all manner of help. ⊠ *125 E. Palace Ave.*

Canyon Road

Canyon Road, nicknamed "the Art and Soul of Santa Fe" because of its many art galleries, shops, and restaurants, stretches for about 2 mi from the eastern curve of Paseo de Peralta.

A Good Walk

Begin on Paseo de Peralta at the **Gerald Peters Gallery** ⑧, and then walk north a half block to **Canyon Road** ⑨. Turn right (east) and follow the road for 2 mi, along the Santa Fe River into the hills above the city. Explore the galleries and shops, and take a break at one of the many fine restaurants. At the intersection of Upper Canyon and Cristo Rey you'll find the massive **Cristo Rey Church** ⑩.

TIMING

A tour of Canyon Road could take a whole day or as little as a few hours. Even on a cold day the walk can be a pleasure, with massive, glistening icicles hanging off roofs and a silence shrouding the side streets. There are few places as festive as Canyon Road on Christmas Eve, when thousands of votive candles shimmer inside brown paper bags on walkways, walls, roofs, and even in trees.

Sights to See

❾ Canyon Road. Once a Native American trail and, during the early part of this century, a route for woodcutters coming into town with their loaded burros, Canyon Road is lined with art galleries that represent artists from around the world. If you're walking, be aware that the road rises at a slight incline. Street parking is at a premium, but there is a lot in the shopping complex at the lower end of Canyon Road and a city-owned pay lot at the corner of Camino del Monte Sol. ⊠ *Canyon Rd. begins along the eastern curve of Paseo de Peralta just south of the Santa Fe River.*

🔟 **Cristo Rey Church.** Built in 1940 to commemorate the 400th anniversary of Francisco Vásquez de Coronado's exploration of the Southwest, this church is the largest adobe structure in the United States and is considered by many the finest example of Pueblo-style architecture anywhere. The church was constructed the old-fashioned way by parishioners, who mixed the more than 200,000 mud-and-straw adobe bricks and hauled them into place. The 225-ton stone reredos (altar screen) is magnificent. ⊠ *1120 Canyon Rd.,* ☎ *505/983–8528.* ☉ *Daily 8–7.*

⑧ **Gerald Peters Gallery.** Santa Fe's premier showcase for 19th- and 20th-century American and European art, formerly located on Canyon Road, celebrated the grand opening of its suavely designed new space in August 1998. Visiting the adobe-style gallery is like going to a museum where all the works are for sale. Georgia O'Keeffe, Charles M. Russell, Deborah Butterfield, George Rickey, and members of the Taos Society are among the artists whose works Gerald Peters represents. ⊠ *1011 Paseo de Peralta,* ☎ *505/954–5700.* 🖾 *Free.* ☉ *Mon.–Sat. 10–5.*

Lower Old Santa Fe Trail

It was along the Old Santa Fe Trail that wagon trains from Missouri rolled into town in the 1800s, forever changing Santa Fe's destiny. This area off the Plaza is one of Santa Fe's most historic.

A Good Walk

The **Loretto Chapel** ⑪, facing the Old Santa Fe Trail, behind the La Fonda hotel (☞ Sante Fe Plaza, *above*), is a good place to start your walk. After visiting the chapel, head southeast on Old Santa Fe Trail to the **San Miguel Mission** ⑫. Across from the Mission, on De Vargas Street, is **the Oldest House** ⑬. Up and down narrow De Vargas stretches the **Barrio de**

Analco ⑭. After exploring this historic street, return to the Old Santa Fe Trail and walk farther away from downtown until you come to the **New Mexico State Capitol** ⑮.

TIMING

Plan on spending a half hour each at the churches and the New Mexico State Capitol and an hour exploring the Barrio de Analco. The entire walk can easily be done in about 3½ hours.

Sights to See

⑭ **Barrio de Analco.** Along the south bank of the Santa Fe River, the barrio—its name means "district on the other side of the water" (in this case the Santa Fe River)—is one of America's oldest neighborhoods, settled in the early 1600s by the Tlaxcalan Indians (who were forbidden to live with the Spanish near the Plaza) and in the 1690s by soldiers who had assisted the Spanish in recapturing New Mexico after the Pueblo Revolt of 1680. Plaques on houses on East De Vargas Street will help you locate some of the important structures.

⑪ **Loretto Chapel.** A delicate Romanesque church modeled after the Sainte-Chapelle chapel in Paris, Loretto was started in 1873 by the same French architects and Italian stonemasons who built Saint Francis Cathedral. The chapel is known for the "Miraculous Staircase" that leads to the choir loft. Legend has it that the chapel was almost finished when it became obvious that there wasn't room enough to complete a staircase to the choir loft. In answer to the prayers of the cathedral's nuns, an old bearded man arrived on a donkey, built a 20-ft staircase—using only a square, a saw, and a tub of water to season the wood—and then disappeared as quickly as he came. Many of the faithful believed it was St. Joseph himself. The staircase contains two complete 360-degree turns with no central support; no nails were used in its construction. The chapel is maintained by the Inn at Loretto (☞ Lodging, *below*), which adjoins it. ⊠ *211 Old Santa Fe Trail*, ☎ *505/984–7971.* ☑ *$2.* ☉ *Mid-Oct.–mid-May, Mon.–Sat. 9–5, Sun. 10:30–5; mid-May–mid-Oct., Mon.–Sat. 8–6, Sun. 10:30–5.*

★ ⑮ **New Mexico State Capitol.** The symbol of the Zía Pueblo, which represents the Circle of Life, was the inspiration for the Capitol, also known as the Roundhouse. Doorways at opposing sides of this 1966 structure symbolize the four winds, the four directions, and the four seasons. Throughout the building are artworks from the outstanding collection of the Capitol Art Foundation, historical and cultural displays, and handcrafted local furniture. Temporary exhibits are presented in the **Governor's Gallery.** Six acres of imaginatively landscaped gardens shelter many outstanding sculptures. ⊠ *Old Santa Fe Trail at Paseo de Peralta,* ☎ *505/ 986–4589.* ▭ *Free.* ☉ *Sept.–May, weekdays 8–5; June– Aug., Mon.–Sat. 8–5; guided tours at 10* AM *and 2* PM.

⑬ The Oldest House. More than 800 years ago Pueblo people built this structure out of "puddled" adobe (liquid mud poured between upright wooden frames), which predates the adobe brick introduced by the Spanish. This house, which contains a gift shop these days, is said to be the most ancient dwelling in the nation. ⊠ *215 E. De Vargas St.*

★ ⑫ San Miguel Mission. The oldest church still in use in the United States, this simple earth-hued adobe structure was built in the early 17th century by the Tlaxcalan Indians of Mexico, who came to New Mexico as servants of the Spanish. Badly damaged in the 1680 Pueblo Revolt, the structure was restored and enlarged in 1710. On display in the chapel are priceless statues and paintings and the San José Bell, weighing nearly 800 pounds, which is believed to have been cast in Spain in 1356 and brought to Santa Fe several centuries later. Mass is held on Sunday at 5 PM. ⊠ *401 Old Santa Fe Trail,* ☎ *505/ 983–3974.* ▭ *$1.* ☉ *May–Oct., Mon.–Sat. 9–4:30, Sun. 3–4:30; Nov.–Apr., Mon–Sat. 10–4, Sun. 3–4:30.*

Upper Old Santa Fe Trail

A Good Tour

This museum tour is best done by car—hearty souls could walk the 2 mi, but it's best to save your energy for exploring the museums. Begin at the **Museum of Indian Arts and Culture** ⑯. To get there from the Plaza, drive uphill on Old Santa Fe Trail to Camino Lejo, a mile past where, heading south, Old Santa Fe Trail veers left at Old Pecos Trail. From the Indian Arts and Culture Museum, cross the parking lot to the **Museum of International Folk Art** ⑰. Nearby is the

Wheelwright Museum of the American Indian ⑱. You'll need to get back in your car and drive back down the hill to reach the **Santa Fe Children's Museum** ⑲.

TIMING

Set aside from four to six hours to see all the museums on the Upper Santa Fe Trail. Kids usually have to be dragged from the Children's Museum, even after an hour or two.

Sights to See

★ ⑯ **Museum of Indian Arts and Culture.** A modern structure, the museum contains some of New Mexico's oldest works of art: pottery vessels, fine stone and silver jewelry, intricate textiles, and other arts and crafts created by Pueblo, Navajo, and Apache artisans. Art demonstrations take place at the museum, and there are interactive displays. A film about the life and work of Pueblo potter Maria Martinez (☞ San Ildefonso Pueblo *in* Side Trips, *below*) is screened. ⊠ *710 Camino Lejo,* ☎ *505/827–6344.* ✍ *$5, 4-day pass $10 (good at the Georgia O'Keeffe museum and all 4 state museums in Santa Fe).* ☉ *Tues.–Sun. 10–5.*

★ ⑰ **Museum of International Folk Art.** Everywhere you look in this facility, the premier institution of its kind in the world, you'll find amazingly inventive handmade objects—a tin Madonna, a devil made from bread dough, and all kinds of rag dolls. Florence Dibell Bartlett, who founded the museum in 1953, donated its first 4,000 works. In the late 1970s Alexander Girard, a designer and architect who with his wife, Susan, was a major folk-art collector, gave the museum 106,000 items. The museum opened its Hispanic Heritage Wing, which contains art dating from the Spanish colonial period (in New Mexico, 1598–1821) to the present, in 1989. The 5,000-piece exhibit includes religious works—particularly *bultos* (carved wooden statues of saints) and *retablos* (holy images painted on wood or tin). The objects in the Neutrogena Wing, which opened in August 1998, are exhibited more by theme than by date or country of origin—you might, for instance, find a sheer Eskimo parka alongside a Chinese undergarment made of bamboo and cotton webbing. Lloyd's Treasure Chest, the wing's innovative basement section, provides a behind-the-scenes look at more of this collection, assembled by Lloyd Cotsen while he headed the Neutrogena Corporation. You can rummage about storage drawers, peer into microscopes, and, on occasion, speak with conservators and other museum personnel. ⊠ *706 Camino Lejo,* ☎ *505/827–6350.* ☞ *$5, 4-day pass $10 (good at the Georgia O'Keeffe Museum and all 4 state museums in Santa Fe).* ☉ *July–Dec., daily 10–5; Jan.–June, Tues.–Sun. 10–5.*

🖐 ⓳ **Santa Fe Children's Museum.** Kids won't be bored at this museum. Stimulating hands-on exhibits, a solar greenhouse, oversize geometric forms, and a simulated 18-ft mountain-climbing wall all contribute to the museum's popularity. Puppeteers and storytellers occasionally perform. ⊠ *1050 Old Pecos Trail,* ☎ *505/989–8359.* ☞ *$3.* ☉ *Sept.–May, Thurs.–Sat. 10–5, Sun. noon–5; June–Aug., Wed.–Sat. 10–5, Sun. noon–5.*

⓲ **Wheelwright Museum of the American Indian.** A private institution in a building shaped like a traditional Navajo hogan, the Wheelwright opened in 1937. Founded by Boston scholar Mary Cabot Wheelwright and Navajo medicine man Hasteen Klah, the museum contains the works of many Native American cultures and mounts impressive special exhibitions. The shop on the lower level is modeled after the trading posts that dotted the southwestern frontier more than 100 years ago. ⊠ *704 Camino Lejo,* ☎ *505/982–4636.* ☞ *Free.* ☉ *Mon.–Sat. 10–5, Sun. 1–5.*

Railroad District

Ten years ago this area at the western edge of downtown Santa Fe was crumbling, but today it is filled with shops, restaurants, and galleries. The highlight of the area is the restored scenic train line, which is once again putting the town's old depot to use.

A Good Walk

Begin at **Santuario de Guadalupe** ⓴, 3½ blocks southwest of the Plaza, at the end of El Camino Real. From the Plaza, head west on San Francisco Street, then head south (take a left) on Guadalupe Street; take your time browsing through the shops and eating lunch in one of the restaurants along the way. At the corner of Montezuma Street turn right and proceed a half block to the end of the railroad tracks on your left, where you'll find one of Santa Fe's two original train stations. If you have time, take the antique train operated by the **Santa Fe Southern Railway** ㉑ to Lamy (18 mi away) and back for stunning views of the distant Ortiz, Sandia, and Jemez mountains. Continue south on Guadalupe to the **SITE Santa Fe** ㉒ gallery and performance space.

TIMING

A visit to the Santuario de Guadalupe can take an hour or so—more if there is an art show in progress. If you like shopping, you might spend hours browsing in the shops on and off Guadalupe Street. The train trip to Lamy and back takes five hours and is best done on a warm, sunny day.

Sights to See

㉑ **Santa Fe Southern Railway.** Antique passenger cars make an 18-mi run from Santa Fe to Lamy. Trains depart from one of Santa Fe's two original train stations, which was once a stop on the "Chile Line" of the Atchison, Topeka & Santa Fe Railway. The tracks extend off the Santa Fe plateau and into the vast Galisteo Basin; views of 120 mi are not uncommon. You can buy lunch in Lamy or pack a picnic. In summer the Sunset Run leaves an hour before dusk and includes a light supper. ⊠ *410 S. Guadalupe St.,* ☎ *800/ 989–8600.* ⌑ *$21; sunset run starts at $45.* ☉ *Departs May– Oct., Tues., Thurs., and weekends about 10:30 AM, returns 2:30–3:30 PM; sunset run departs anywhere from 6 PM to 7:15 PM. Call for winter schedule and sunset run times.*

㉒ **Santuario de Guadalupe.** A humble adobe structure built by Franciscan missionaries between 1776 and 1795, this is the oldest shrine in the United States to Our Lady of Guadalupe, patron saint of Mexico. The shrine, now a nonprofit cultural center, has adobe walls nearly 3 ft thick. Among the paintings on exhibit is a priceless 16th-century work by Venetian painter Leonardo de Ponte Bassano that depicts Jesus driving the money changers from the temple. Also of note is a portrait of Our Lady of Guadalupe by the Mexican colonial painter José de Alzíbar. Other highlights are an authentic 19th-century sacristy, a pictorial-history archive, a library devoted to Archbishop Jean Baptiste Lamy that is furnished with many of his belongings, and a garden with plants from the Holy Land. ⊠ *100 Guadalupe St.,* ☎ *505/988–2027.* ⌑ *Donation suggested.* ☉ *May– Oct., Mon.–Sat. 9–4; Nov.–Apr., weekdays 9–4.*

SITE Santa Fe. The events at this nexus of artistic activity include lectures, concerts, author readings, performance art, and gallery shows. The facility hosts a biennial exhibition every odd-numbered year. ⊠ *1606 Paseo de Peralta,* ☎ *505/ 989–1199.* ▨ *$2.50, free Sun.–Mon.* ☉ *Daily 10–5.*

DINING

Santa Fe cuisine is a robust mixture of Pueblo, Spanish, Mexican, and Continental influences. Chefs at cheerful cafés prepare superb Mexican dishes; nouvelle New Mexican cuisine is served at elegant restaurants; and you can even go downscale for hamburgers and comfort food.

CATEGORY	COST*
$$$$	over $30
$$$	$20–$30
$$	$10–$20
$	under $10

per person, excluding drinks, service, and sales tax (6.25%)

American

$$$– $$$$ ✕ **El Nido.** Since the 1920s, Santa Feans have made the 6-mi drive to the village of Tesuque to eat at this former dance hall and trading post, which has a cozy ambience and a solid menu of choice aged beef, fresh seafood, and local specialties like the chunky green-chile stew. Only a five-minute drive from the Santa Fe Opera, El Nido is a favorite of opera fans. ⊠ *U.S. 285/84 (6 mi north of Santa Fe to first Tesuque Exit, then about ¼ mi farther to restaurant),* ☎ *505/988–4340. AE, MC, V. Closed Mon.*

$$$– $$$$ ✕ **Vanessie.** Everything is oversize at Vanessie's, where beef, chicken, fish, and rack of lamb come with jumbo baked potatoes. The salads are enormous—even the onion-loaf appetizer is gargantuan. Beamed ceilings and massive oak tables with high-back chairs create a lodgelike ambience. After dinner amble over to the piano bar, a perfect place to sit, listen to wistful tunes, and digest all that food. ⊠ *434 W. San Francisco St.,* ☎ *505/982–9966. AE, DC, MC, V.*

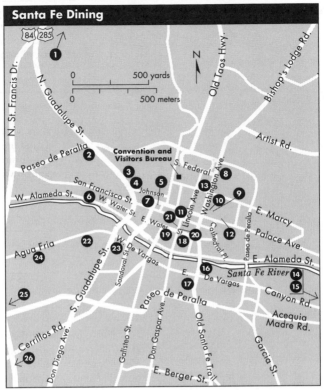

Santa Fe Dining

Anasazi, **10**

Bert's Burger Bowl, **3**

Bistro 315, **16**

Cafe Pasqual's, **20**

Cowgirl Hall of Fame, **23**

Coyote Cafe, **19**

Dave's Not Here, **25**

El Farol, **14**

El Nido, **1**

Geronimo, **15**

Il Piatto, **13**

India Palace, **18**

La Casa Sena, **12**

La Tertulia, **22**

Old House, **7**

Old Mexico Grill, **26**

Ore House on the Plaza, **11**

The Palace, **5**

Pink Adobe, **17**

Plaza Café, **21**

Ristra, **24**

Santacafé, **8**

The Shed, **9**

Shohko, **4**

Vanessie, **6**

Whistling Moon Cafe, **2**

American/Casual

$$ ✕ **Plaza Café.** Run with homespun care by the Razatos
★ family since 1947, this café has been a fixture on the
Plaza since 1918. From all appearances, the decor—red
leather banquettes, black Formica tables, tile floors, vin-
tage Santa Fe photos, a coffered tin ceiling, and a 1940s-
style service counter—hasn't changed much in the past half
century. Standard American fare like hamburgers and
tuna sandwiches is served, along with New Mexican and
Greek dishes. A bowl of green chile and beans will leave
your tongue burning—that's the way the locals like it. You
can cool it off, though, with an old-fashioned ice cream
treat from the soda fountain or a towering slice of coconut-
cream pie. There's a good beer and wine selection. ⊠ *54
Lincoln Ave.,* ☎ *505/982–1664. Reservations not ac-
cepted. AE, D, MC, V.*

$–$$ ✕ **Bert's Burger Bowl.** Since the 1950s this tiny place has
been serving up yummy charbroiled burgers—the No. 6
(green chile with cheese) is a staple. You can also get excellent pressure-cooked chicken, *carne adovada* (red chile-
marinated pork), crispy fries, and old-fashioned shakes.
There are tables outside and a few chairs indoors. ⊠ *235
N. Guadalupe St.,* ☎ *505/982–0215. No credit cards.*

$ ✕ **Dave's Not Here.** Dave may not be here, but you will
find one of Santa Fe's best burgers, served with heaps of
onions, mushrooms, avocado, or cheese. The cooks at
Dave's prepare super made-from-scratch chiles rellenos. For
dessert try the slab of deep chocolate cake. ⊠ *1115 Hickox
St. (the extension of Paseo de Peralta west from St. Francis Dr.),* ☎ *505/983–7060. Reservations not accepted. No
credit cards.*

Contemporary

$$$$ ✕ **Bistro 315.** More like a place you'd find on a thor-
oughfare in Paris than on the Old Santa Fe Trail, Bistro 315
has a trendy decor. Chef Matt Yohalem prepares bistro fare
using organic vegetables, locally raised beef and lamb, free-
range chicken, and fresh seafood. Seasonal specialties on
the ever-evolving menu might include duckling with creamy
polenta and wild mushrooms, or stuffed Portobello mush-

rooms served with a potato *galette* (flat cake). In good weather you can dine on the patio. ⊠ *315 Old Santa Fe Trail,* ☏ *505/986–9190. Reservations essential. AE, MC, V. Closed Sun.–Mon. in winter.*

$$$$
★ ✕ **Coyote Cafe.** The Coyote's bright modern room and sprightly menu are the creations of chef-owner Mark Miller. Try "The Cowboy," a 22-ounce rib-eye steak served with barbecued black beans and onion rings dusted with red chile, the squash-blossom and corn-cake appetizers, or the ravioli filled with sausage made of wild boar and goat cheese. On the wine list are more than 500 vintages. In summer the Rooftop Cantina serves equally exotic but less expensive dishes like duck quesadillas. The Coyote General Store, under the café, sells Southwestern foodstuffs and Miller's cookbooks. ⊠ *132 W. Water St.,* ☏ *505/983–1615. Reservations essential. AE, D, DC, MC, V.*

$$$$
★ ✕ **Old House.** Chef Martin Rios changes the menu every Thursday at his fashionably casual restaurant inside the equally fashionable Eldorado Hotel. Past entrées have included barbecued breast of quail on a crispy corn cake and rack of lamb in a pepita-garlic crust. More than two dozen of the impressive wines are served by the glass. ⊠ *Eldorado Hotel, 309 W. San Francisco St.,* ☏ *505/988–4455. Reservations essential during the summer and on weekends year-round. AE, D, DC, MC, V. Closed Mon. No lunch.*

$$$–
$$$$ ✕ **Ore House on the Plaza.** Popular more for its perfect location overlooking the Plaza than for its cuisine, this restaurant serves salmon, swordfish, lobster, ceviche, and steaks that are adequate if uninspired. The specialty margaritas, though, are anything but ordinary: They come in more than 80 flavors, from cool watermelon to zippy jalapeño. ⊠ *50 Lincoln Ave., upstairs on the southwest corner of the Plaza,* ☏ *505/983–8687. AE, MC, V.*

$$$–
$$$$ ✕ **Ristra.** Navajo blankets hang on stark white walls and Pueblo pottery adorns a handful of niches in this minimalist space where Continental dishes—mussels in *chipotle* (a hot, smoky chile) and mint broth, rack of lamb with creamed garlic potatoes, and perfectly grilled salmon—receive Southwestern accents. The wines are well selected and the service is swift and courteous. ⊠ *548 Agua Fria St.,* ☏ *505/ 982–8608. AE, D, MC, V. No lunch.*

Eclectic

$$$–   ✕ **Pink Adobe.** Rosalea Murphey has owned this restau-
$$$$ rant for 50 years. The several dining rooms have fireplaces
and works by artists that include Rosalea herself. The steak
Dunnigan, smothered in green chile and mushrooms, and
the savory shrimp Louisianne—deep-fried and crispy—are
among the perennial Continental, New Orleans Creole, and
New Mexican dishes served here. The apple pie drenched
in rum sauce is a perennial favorite. The menu is more lim-
ited in the adjacent Dragon Room bar. ⊠ *406 Old Santa
Fe Trail,* ☎ *505/983–7712. AE, D, DC, MC, V. No lunch
weekends.*

Indian

$$ ✕ **India Palace.** East Indian cuisine was utterly foreign to
most locals before the arrival of Indian Palace, but many
Santa Feans have since become devotees of chef Bal Dev
Singh's spicy dishes. The serene deep-pink interior sets the
scene for tender tandoori chicken and lamb and superb cur-
ried seafood and vegetables. Meals are cooked as hot or
mild as you wish, and vegetarian dishes are prepared. ⊠
*227 Don Gaspar Ave. (at the rear of the El Centro shop-
ping compound across the Water St. parking lot from the
Hotel St. Francis),* ☎ *505/986–5859. AE, D, MC, V.*

Italian

$$$–   ✕ **The Palace.** One of New Mexico's premier restaurants,
$$$$ a real power-lunching hub, the Palace has upholstered ban-
quettes and a saloon with rich red wallpaper (a remnant
from the days of Doña Tules, a famed madam and gam-
bling tycoon who owned the building in the 1800s). The
present owner, Lino Pertusini, is from Italy and he focuses
on Italian and Continental cuisine. Try the sautéed sweet-
breads, the linguine with shrimp, and the irresistible pas-
tries. The wine list is fine, the service professional. In
summer there's patio dining. ⊠ *142 W. Palace Ave.,* ☎ *505/
982–9891. AE, D, MC, V. No lunch Sun.*

$$–$$$ ✕ **Il Piatto.** The owners of Bistro 315 opened this Italian
restaurant, which serves creative pasta dishes like risotto
with duck, artichoke, and truffle oil, and homemade pump-

kin ravioli. Entrées include pancetta-wrapped trout with rosemary and lemon, and roast chicken with Italian sausage, potatoes, peppers, and onions. ⊠ *95 W. Marcy,* ☎ *505/984– 1091. AE, DC, MC, V. No lunch Sat. or Sun.*

Japanese

$$–$$$ ✕ **Shohko.** Tasty tempura—including a Southwestern variation made with green chile—and more than 35 kinds of sushi are on the menu at this small Japanese restaurant. If possible, sit at the 16-seat sushi bar and watch the masters at work. ⊠ *321 Johnson St.,* ☎ *505/983–7288. AE, D, MC, V.*

Mediterranean

$$–$$$ ✕ **Whistling Moon Cafe.** Unusual spices scent the Mediterranean fare served at Whistling Moon. The menu includes pasta calamari, Greek salad, a Middle Eastern sampler, and grilled duck. The coriander-cumin fries are irresistible, as is the homemade Greek honey cheesecake. Although the small ocher dining room with red Moroccan weavings is a touch noisy, the food and prices more than make up for it. There's also patio dining in season. ⊠ *402 N. Guadalupe St.,* ☎ *505/ 983–3093. Reservations essential for 6 or more. MC, V.*

Southwestern

$$$$ ✕ **Anasazi.** A soft light illuminates the stone and adobe in-
★ terior of this restaurant, which became a Santa Fe fixture the day it opened. Chef John Bobrick combines New Mexican and Native American flavors to produce exotic fare like flat bread with fire-roasted sweet peppers, and cinnamon-chile tenderloin of beef with chipotle, white-cheddar mashed potatoes, and mango salsa. The large dining room has wooden tables and *bancos* (banquettes) upholstered with handwoven textiles from Chimayó. Groups of up to 12 can dine in the private wine cellar, and groups of up to 40 can be served in the library. ⊠ *113 Washington Ave.,* ☎ *505/ 988–3030. AE, D, DC, MC, V.*

$$$$ ✕ **Cafe Pasqual's.** A block southwest of the Plaza, this cheerful cubbyhole of a restaurant dishes up regional specialties and possibly the best breakfast in town—served all day. Forget the pancakes and order a chorizo burrito (eggs scrambled with ground Mexican sausage and potatoes, wrapped in a whole wheat tortilla, and topped with New Mexican chile and cheese) or the succulent corned-beef hash. For dinner there's chile-rubbed pan-roasted salmon with a tomatillo-avocado salsa and chile-corn pudding. Piñatas, *ristras* (strings of red chile peppers), ceramic pottery, and huge colorful murals set a festive tone. Expect a line at breakfast and lunch. ⊠ *121 Don Gaspar Ave.,* ☎ *505/983–9340 or 800/722–7672. AE, MC, V.*

$$$$ ✕ **Geronimo.** Chef Eric DiStefano changes the menu frequently at this restaurant in the Borrego House, which
★ dates from 1756. A typical meal might include mesquite-grilled elk tenderloin with scallion risotto or red-corn relleno with duck and black-bean sauce. The Sunday brunch is also impressive. The intimate, white dining rooms have beamed ceilings, wood floors, fireplaces, and cushioned bancos. In summer you can dine under the front portal; in winter the bar and fireplace are inviting. ⊠ *724 Canyon Rd.,* ☎ *505/982–1500. AE, MC, V. No lunch Mon.*

$$$$ ✕ **La Casa Sena.** The Southwestern and Continental fare served at La Casa Sena is delicious. If you order the *trucha en terra-cotta* (fresh trout wrapped in corn husks and baked in clay), ask your waiter to save the clay head for you as a souvenir. Finish dinner with the wonderful citrus mascarpone tart with orange sauce and Grand Marnier–soaked berries. The more than 700 wines stocked here earned the restaurant *Wine Spectator* magazine's Award of Excellence. For a musical meal (evenings only) sit in the restaurant's adjacent Cantina, where staff members belt out Broadway show tunes. ⊠ *Sena Plaza, 125 E. Palace Ave.,* ☎ *505/988–9232. AE, D, DC, MC, V.*

$$$$ ✕ **Santacafé.** Floral bouquets decorate the thick adobe
★ walls of this romantic restaurant—one of Santa Fe's finest—two blocks north of the Plaza in the historic Padre Gallegos House. The shrimp and spinach dumplings with tahini sauce, and the shiitake mushrooms and cactus spring rolls are particularly good. The patio is a joy in summer. ⊠ *231 Washington Ave.,* ☎ *505/984–1788. AE, MC, V.*

$$–$$$$ ✕ **La Tertulia.** In a converted 19th-century convent, this restaurant, which contains a splendid Spanish-colonial art collection, serves good New Mexican cuisine. Among the culinary highlights are tender carne adovada, *chalupas* (bowl-shape corn tortillas filled with beans, chicken, or beef), and flan. The tangy sangria is extraordinary. ⊠ *416 Agua Fria St.,* ☎ *505/988–2769. AE, D, DC, MC, V. Closed Mon.*

$$–$$$ ✕ **Old Mexico Grill.** For a taste of Old Mexico in New Mex-
★ ico, sample dishes like *arracheras* (the traditional name for fajitas—grilled beef, chicken, or fish with peppers and onions and served with tortillas), and tacos *al carbón* (shredded pork cooked in a mole sauce and folded into corn tortillas). Start the meal with a fresh ceviche appetizer and a cool lime margarita. The restaurant's location in a shopping center makes parking a snap. ⊠ *2434 Cerrillos Rd., College Plaza S,* ☎ *505/473–0338. Reservations not accepted. D, MC, V. No lunch weekends.*

$$–$$$ ✕ **The Shed.** The lines at lunch attest to the favored status among Santa Feans of this downtown New Mexican eatery. In a rambling adobe dating from 1692, the restaurant is decorated with festive folk art, and its service is downright neighborly. Specialties include red-chile enchiladas, green-chile stew with potatoes and pork, *posole* (soup made with lime hominy, pork, chile, and garlic), and charbroiled "Shedburgers." The homemade desserts are fabulous. ⊠ *113½ E. Palace Ave.,* ☎ *505/982–9030. Reservations accepted only for parties of six or more. AE, DC, MC, V. Closed Sun. No dinner Mon.–Wed.*

$–$$$ ✕ **Cowgirl Hall of Fame.** Part restaurant, part bar, part museum, and part theater, this fun place serves Texas-style brisket and barbecue and good New Mexican fare, including tasty chiles rellenos, grilled-salmon soft tacos, and butternut-squash casserole. In summer you can dine on tree-shaded patios, and kids can eat in the Corral, a special area with its own menu. After dinner there's entertainment— blues and rock bands, singer-songwriters, or comedians. ⊠ *319 S. Guadalupe St.,* ☎ *505/982–2565. AE, D, MC, V.*

Spanish

$$–$$$ ✕ **El Farol.** Owner David Salazar sums up his food in one word: "Spanish." Order a classic entrée like paella or make a meal from the 20 different tapas—from tiny fried squid to wild mushrooms. Dining is indoors and outdoors at relaxed El Farol. People push back the chairs and start danc-

ing at around 9:30. ✉ *808 Canyon Rd.,* ☎ *505/983–9912. D, DC, MC, V.*

LODGING

You can go downscale or upscale in Santa Fe, from no-frills motels on Cerrillos Road to historic hotels in the heart of town to luxurious resorts in the foothills to the north. There are also many bed-and-breakfasts and campgrounds. Because Santa Fe is a tourist destination, hotel prices can be high. Rates become lower in the off-season, from November to April (excluding Thanksgiving and Christmas).

CATEGORY	COST*
$$$$	over $150
$$$	$100–$150
$$	$65–$100
$	under $65

All prices are for a standard double room, excluding tax (5.8%), in peak season.

Downtown Santa Fe

$$$$ 🏨 **Eldorado Hotel.** The city's largest hotel, a too-modern affair for some visitors, is in the heart of downtown, not far from the Plaza. Rooms are stylishly furnished with art prints, carved, Southwestern-style desks and chairs, and large upholstered club chairs. Many rooms have terraces or kiva-style fireplaces. Baths are spacious and completely tiled. The Old House Restaurant, which serves contemporary Continental cuisine, is highly rated. There's music nightly in the bar. ✉ *309 W. San Francisco St., 87501,* ☎ *505/988–4455 or 800/955–4455,* 🖷 *505/995–4544. 201 rooms, 18 suites, and 19 casitas (including 8 condos). 2 restaurants, bar, pool, hot tub, sauna, health club, shops, concierge, convention center, meeting rooms, valet parking. AE, D, DC, MC, V.*

$$$$ 🏨 **Hotel Loretto.** Also known as the Inn at Loretto, this refurbished landmark next to the Loretto Chapel was modeled after a multistory Pueblo structure—the doors, windows, light fixtures, and other architectural elements replicate 13th-century designs. Plush Santa Fe–style furnishings decorate the rooms. ✉ *211 Old Santa Fe Trail, 87501,* ☎ *505/*

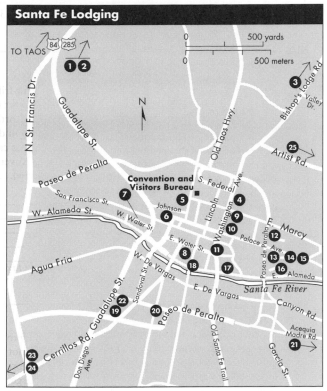

Santa Fe Lodging

TO TAOS

500 yards

500 meters

N

Convention and Visitors Bureau

Alexander's Inn, **15**

Bishop's Lodge, **3**

Dunshee's, **21**

El Rey Inn, **23**

Eldorado Hotel, **6**

Grant Corner Inn, **5**

Hacienda del Cerezo, **2**

Hotel Loretto, **17**

Hotel Plaza Real, **9**

Hotel St. Francis, **8**

Hotel Santa Fe, **19**

Inn of the Anasazi, **10**

Inn of the Animal Tracks, **12**

Inn of the Governors, **18**

Inn on the Alameda, **16**

La Fonda, **11**

La Posada de Santa Fe, **13**

Motel 6, **24**

Preston House, **14**

Pueblo Bonito B&B Inn, **20**

Rancho Encantado, **1**

Santa Fe Motel, **22**

Ten Thousand Waves/Houses of the Moon, **25**

Territorial Inn, **4**

Water Street Inn, **7**

988–5531 or 800/528–1234 outside NM, ᖴ᙭ 505/989–
7968. 143 rooms. Restaurant, lounge, pool, beauty salon,
shops. AE, D, DC, MC, V.

$$$$ ⚄ **Hotel Plaza Real.** Handcrafted Southwestern furniture
decorates the large rooms, all off an interior brick courtyard, at the handsome brick-trimmed Territorial-style Plaza
Real. Most rooms have patios or balconies and wood-
burning fireplaces. ⊠ 125 Washington Ave., 87501, ☎ 505/
988–4900 or 800/537–8483, ᖴ᙭ 505/983–9322. 56 rooms
and suites. Coffee shop, lounge. AE, D, DC, MC, V.

$$$$ ⚄ **Hotel Santa Fe.** Picurís Pueblo maintains the controlling
interest in this Pueblo-style three-story hotel. Rooms and
suites are decorated in traditional Southwestern style, with
locally handmade furniture and Pueblo paintings (Picurís
means "those who paint"), many by Gerald Nailor. All suites
have microwave ovens. The hotel gift shop, the only trib-
ally owned store in Santa Fe, has lower prices than many
nearby retail stores. ⊠ 1501 Paseo de Peralta, 87505, ☎
505/982–1200 or 800/825–9876 outside NM, ᖴ᙭ 505/983–
0785. 40 rooms, 91 suites. Restaurant, pool, hot tub. AE,
D, DC, MC, V.

$$$$ ⚄ **Inn of the Anasazi.** In the heart of the historic district,
★   this hotel is one of Santa Fe's finest. Each room has a
beamed ceiling, kiva-style fireplace, and handcrafted furniture. Extras include a personal attendant who acts as a
concierge, twice-daily maid service, room delivery of exercise bikes upon request, and a library with books on
New Mexico and the Southwest. The Anasazi Restaurant
serves Native American and cowboy cuisine. ⊠ 113 Washington Ave., 87501, ☎ 505/988–3030 or 800/688–8100,
ᖴ᙭ 505/988–3277. 59 rooms and suites. Restaurant, in-room
safes, minibars, in-room VCRs. AE, D, DC, MC, V.

$$$$ ⚄ **Inn of the Governors.** The intimate lobby and gracious
service at this hotel two blocks from the Plaza will quickly
make you feel at home. The standard rooms have a Mexican theme, with bright colors, hand-painted folk art, Southwestern fabrics, and handmade furnishings; deluxe rooms
also have balconies and fireplaces. New Mexican dishes and
lighter fare like wood-oven pizzas are served in the dining
room. ⊠ 234 Don Gaspar Ave. (at Alameda), 87501, ☎
505/982–4333 or 800/234–4534, ᖴ᙭ 505/989–9149. 100
rooms. Piano bar, pool, free parking. AE, D, DC, MC, V.

$$$$ **Inn on the Alameda.** Nestled between the Santa Fe Plaza and Canyon Road is one of the city's best small hotels. Alameda means "tree-lined lane," and this one perfectly complements the inn's riverside location. The adobe architecture and enclosed courtyards combine a relaxed New Mexico country atmosphere with the luxury and amenities of a top-notch hotel. Rooms have a Southwestern color scheme and handmade armoires, headboards, and ceramic lamps and tiles. ⊠ *303 E. Alameda St., 87501,* ☎ *505/984–2121 or 800/289–2122,* FAX *505/986–8325. 69 rooms and suites. Bar, refrigerators, 2 hot tubs, exercise room. Full breakfast. AE, D, DC, MC, V.*

$$$$ **La Fonda.** When Santa Fe was established in 1610 the
 ★   town already had an adobe fonda to accommodate travelers. Two centuries later the original hotel was still welcoming guests—traders, trappers, mountain men, soldiers, and politicians. The present structure, built in 1922 and enlarged many times since, is the only lodging directly on the Plaza, and probably the only hotel anywhere that has hosted both Kit Carson and John F. Kennedy. Antiques and Native American art decorate the tiled lobby. Each room has hand-decorated wood furniture, wrought-iron light fixtures, and beamed ceilings; some of the suites have fireplaces. Bands—from country and folk to flamenco and Latin jazz—play nightly in the bar. ⊠ *100 E. San Francisco St., 87501,* ☎ *505/982–5511 or 800/523–5002 outside NM,* FAX *505/988–2952. 143 rooms, 24 suites. Restaurant, bar, pool, 2 hot tubs, meeting rooms, parking (fee). AE, D, DC, MC, V.*

$$$$ **La Posada de Santa Fe.** Two blocks from the Plaza, this hotel sits on 6 acres of landscaped gardens and lawns shaded by giant elms, fruit trees, and cottonwoods. Some rooms have fireplaces, beamed ceilings, and Native American rugs. The Staab House Restaurant serves up a great Sunday brunch and has a romantic bar. ⊠ *330 E. Palace Ave., 87501,* ☎ *505/986–0000 or 800/727–5276,* FAX *505/982–6850. 119 rooms and suites. Restaurant, bar, pool, free parking. AE, D, DC, MC, V.*

$$$–   **Territorial Inn.** Creature comforts are a high priority at
$$$$ this 1890s brick structure, set back off a busy downtown street two blocks from the Plaza. The well-maintained rooms have Victorian decors; No. 9 has a canopied bed and

a fireplace. Afternoon treats and brandy-and-cookie night-caps are among the extras. ⊠ *215 Washington Ave., 87501,* ☎ *505/989–7737,* F𝖠X *505/986–9212. 10 rooms, 8 with bath, 2 with shared bath. Hot tub, free parking. Continental breakfast. AE, DC, MC, V.*

$$$–
$$$$
★
🏨 **Water Street Inn.** The large rooms in this restored adobe 2½ blocks from the Plaza are decorated with reed shutters, pine antique beds, hand-stenciled paintings, and a blend of cowboy, Hispanic, and Native American art and artifacts. Most have fireplaces; all have private baths, VCRs, cable TV, phones, and voice mail. Afternoon hors d'oeuvres are served in the living room. ⊠ *427 W. Water St., 87501,* ☎ *505/984–1193 or 800/646–6752. 12 rooms. Free parking. Continental breakfast. AE, DC, MC, V.*

$$–$$$$
★
🏨 **Alexander's Inn.** This two-story 1903 Craftsman-style house in the Eastside residential area, a few blocks from the Plaza and Canyon Road, exudes the charm of an old country inn. Rooms have American country–style wooden furnishings and flower arrangements. There are also two two-story cottages ideal for bigger groups, and the adobe-style Casa de Flores, which has a Mexican-tile kitchen. At press time, the owners of Alexander's Inn had purchased the nearby Preston House (☞ *below*). ⊠ *529 E. Palace Ave., 87501,* ☎ *505/986–1431. 12 rooms, 10 with bath; 4 cottages. Hot tub. Full breakfast. MC, DC, V.*

$$–$$$$
🏨 **Preston House.** The only Queen Anne house in the city is three blocks east of the Plaza in a quiet garden setting. The public rooms are open and sunny; fruit bowls, original and fantastically futuristic stained-glass windows, lace curtains, and fresh-cut flowers are all part of the appeal of this place, where you'll feel you've made a genteel step back in time. Rooms in the main home are furnished in ornate late–19th-century fashion. At press time, the owners of Alexander's Inn (☞ *above*) had purchased Preston House. ⊠ *106 Faithway St., 87501,* ☎ F𝖠X *505/982–3465 or* ☎ *800/877–7622. 8 rooms, 6 with bath. Continental breakfast. AE, MC, V.*

$$$
🏨 **Dunshee's.** So romantic that its patio has been used for weddings, this B&B is in the quiet Eastside area a mile from the Plaza. You have two options: One is a suite in the restored adobe home of artist Susan Dunshee, the proprietor; the other, good for families, is an adobe casita. The suite has a living room, a bedroom with a queen bed, kiva-style

BONUS MILES MAKE
GREAT SOUVENIRS.

Earn Miles With Your MCI Card.

Take the MCI Card along on this trip and start earning miles for the next one. You'll earn frequent flyer miles on all your calls and save with the low rates you've come to expect from MCI. Before you know it, you'll be on your way to some other international destination.

Sign up for MCI by calling 1-800-FLY-FREE

Is this a great time, or what? :-)

Earn Frequent Flyer Miles.

AmericanAirlines®
A'Advantage®

Continental Airlines
OnePass

▲ Delta Air Lines
SkyMiles®

HAWAIIAN
AIRLINES.

MIDWEST EXPRESS AIRLINES

NORTHWEST AIRLINES
WORLDPERKS®

Rapid Rewards™
SOUTHWEST AIRLINES®

MILEAGE PLUS.
United Airlines

US AIRWAYS
DIVIDEND MILES

fireplaces, and viga ceilings, and is decorated with antiques and works by area artists. The casita has two bedrooms, a living room, a patio, a completely equipped and stocked kitchen, a kiva-style fireplace, and is adorned with decorative linens and folk art. ⊠ *986 Acequia Madre, 87501,* ☎ *505/982–0988. 1 suite, 1 small house. Continental breakfast. MC, V.*

$$$ 🏠 **Grant Corner Inn.** Though this B&B is downtown, the surrounding small garden and portal make it feel private. Antique Spanish and American country furnishings share space with potted greens and knickknacks. Room accents include old-fashioned fixtures, quilts, and Native American blankets. The ample breakfast, which is open to the public, includes home-baked breads and pastries, jellies, and blue-corn waffles. ⊠ *122 Grant Ave., 87501,* ☎ *505/983–6678,* ℻ *505/983–1526. 9 rooms, 2 share bath, 1 minisuite, 2 rooms in nearby hacienda. Full breakfast. DC, MC, V.*

$$$ 🏠 **Hotel St. Francis.** Listed in the National Register of Historic Places, this three-story building, parts of which were
★ constructed in 1920, has walkways lined with turn-of-the-century lampposts. In a prime location a block south of the Plaza, the hotel contains simple rooms with high ceilings, casement windows, brass-and-iron beds, marble and cherry antiques, and original artworks. Many rooms have hand-painted armoires. Afternoon tea, with scones and finger sandwiches, is served daily in the huge lobby, which rises 50 ft from a floor of blood-red tiles. The St. Francis Club, which has the feel of an English hunt club, serves Continental cuisine. The hotel bar is among the few places in town where you can grab a bite to eat until midnight. ⊠ *210 Don Gaspar Ave., 87501,* ☎ *505/983–5700 or 800/529–5700,* ℻ *505/989–7690. 82 rooms. Restaurant, bar, free parking. AE, D, DC, MC, V.*

$$$ 🏠 **Pueblo Bonito B&B Inn.** Rooms in this aging adobe compound that was built in 1873 contain handmade and hand-painted furnishings, Navajo weavings, sand paintings and pottery, locally carved santos, and Western art. All have fireplaces, and many have kitchens. Breakfast is served in the main dining room. ⊠ *138 W. Manhattan Ave., 87501,* ☎ *505/984–8001 or 800/461–4599,* ℻ *505/984–3155. 11 rooms, 7 suites. Coin laundry. Continental breakfast. AE, DC, MC, V.*

$$–$$$ ⚏ **Inn of the Animal Tracks.** This restored Pueblo-style home three blocks east of the Plaza has beamed ceilings, hardwood floors, handcrafted furniture, and fireplaces. Each guest room is decorated with an animal theme, such as Soaring Eagle or Gentle Deer. Be prepared for cuteness: The Whimsical Rabbit Room, for instance, is filled with stuffed and terra-cotta rabbit statues, rabbit books, rabbit drawings. You'll even find bunny-rabbit slippers under the bed. (This room opens directly onto the kitchen, where the cook arrives at 6 AM.) In summer the backyard is delightful, and in-room air-conditioning provides respite from the rare hot days in Santa Fe. ⊠ *707 Paseo de Peralta, 87504,* ☎ *505/988–1546,* FAX *505/982–8098. 5 rooms. Full breakfast. MC, V.*

$$ ⚏ **El Rey Inn.** As nice a motel as you'll find anywhere, the tree-shaded El Rey consists of whitewashed buildings with tile trim. Rooms are decorated in Southwestern, Spanish colonial, and Victorian style. Some have kitchenettes and fireplaces. The largest suite, with seven rooms, sleeps six and has antique furniture, a full kitchen, a breakfast nook, and two patios. ⊠ *1862 Cerrillos Rd., 87501,* ☎ *505/982–1931 or 800/521–1349,* FAX *505/989–9249. 79 rooms, 8 suites. Kitchenettes, pool, 2 hot tubs, sauna, playground, coin laundry. Continental breakfast. AE, DC, MC, V.*

$$ ⚏ **Santa Fe Motel.** Proximity is a prime asset of this property—an unusually successful upgrade of a standard motel—which is within walking distance from the Plaza. Rooms, some with kitchenettes, are decorated in contemporary Southwestern style. ⊠ *510 Cerrillos Rd., 87501,* ☎ *505/982–1039 or 800/999–1039,* FAX *505/986–1275. 13 rooms, 8 casitas. AE, MC, V.*

$ ⚏ **Motel 6.** The amenities at this well-maintained chain property several miles from the Plaza include an outdoor pool, free HBO, and free local calls. Those under 17 stay free with parents. ⊠ *3007 Cerrillos Rd., 87505,* ☎ *505/473–1380,* FAX *505/473–7784. 104 rooms. Pool. AE, DC, MC, V.*

North of Santa Fe

$$$$ ⚏ **Bishop's Lodge.** In a bucolic valley at the foot of the San-
★ gre de Cristo Mountains only five minutes by car from the Plaza, this resort established in 1918 feels far removed

from the hustle and bustle of town. Behind the main building is an exquisite chapel, open for visitation, that was once the private retreat of Archbishop Jean Baptiste Lamy. Outdoor activities include horseback riding, organized trail riding (with meals) into the adjacent national forest, skeet-shooting, and trapshooting. Guest rooms and public spaces in the one- and three-story lodges have old Southwestern furnishings—shipping chests, tinwork from Mexico, and Native American and Western art. A bountiful brunch, probably the best in the area, is served on Sunday. ⊠ *Bishop's Lodge Rd., 87504, ☎ 505/983–6377 or 800/ 732–2240, ℻ 505/989–8739. 70 rooms, 18 suites. Bar, pool, hot tub, spa, 4 tennis courts, exercise room, hiking, horseback riding, fishing, airport shuttle, free parking. AE, D, MC, V.*

$$$$ ⚏ **Hacienda del Cerezo.** A superbly detailed high-end inn,
★ Hacienda del Cerezo rests on a splendidly isolated patch of land 25 minutes north of downtown. The rooms have different themes (sun, corn, fans), subtly executed in prints, ornaments, engravings on the beams of the viga ceilings, and etchings in the glass shower doors. Each room has a king-size bed, a generous sitting area, a kiva fireplace, an enclosed patio, and a fine view of the mountains. The bathrooms are sumptuous. The rates include three meals prepared by a master chef; dinner is a five-course candlelit affair in the high-ceiling great room or in the courtyard, looking out onto the vanishing-edge pool and the desert beyond. Staying here is like being the houseguest of a gracious family; the hacienda's remoteness makes it an ideal spot to get far, far away from it all, and the high tariff assures exclusivity. ⊠ *100 Camino del Cerezo, 87501, ☎ 505/982–8000 or 888/982–8001, ℻ 505/983–7162. 10 rooms. Pool, outdoor hot tub, tennis court, hiking, horseback riding. American Plan.*

$$$$ ⚏ **Rancho Encantado.** Robert Redford, Johnny Cash, Robert
★ Plant, and the Dalai Lama are among the past guests of this resort on 168 acres. The accommodations have Southwestern-style furniture, handmade and hand-painted by local craftspeople, in addition to fine Spanish and Western pieces from the 1850s and earlier. Some of the villas and rooms have fireplaces, private patios, and tiled floors; others have carpeting and refrigerators. The dining room,

with a terrific view of the Jemez Mountains, serves good Continental fare. ✉ *NM 4; 8 mi north of Santa Fe off U.S. 84/285 near Tesuque, on NM 592 (Box 57C), 87501, ☎ 505/982–3537 or 800/722–9339, ℻ 505/983–8269. 29 rooms, 29 villas. 2 pools, hot tub, 2 tennis courts, hiking. AE, D, DC, MC, V.*

$$$ ⊞ **Ten Thousand Waves/Houses of the Moon.** Santa Fe
★ style gives way to Japanese manner in the moonlit mountains 4 mi above town at this health spa and miniresort. You can choose from five small houses, which are on a hillside and reached by a path through piñons. All have brick floors, marble fireplaces, and adobe-color walls, plus Japanese art, fine woodwork, and futon beds; two come with full kitchens. If you are staying overnight, you get 10% off all services at the spa—the perfect place to unwind after a day's cavorting. The facility has private and communal indoor and outdoor hot tubs; treatments include therapeutic massages, facials, and herbal wraps. Towels, kimonos, soaps, shampoos, sandals, and lockers are provided. Tubs run from $18 to $25 per hour; massage and spa treatments cost from $35 to $120. ✉ *4 mi from the Plaza on road to Santa Fe Ski Basin (Box 10200), 87504, ☎ 505/982–9304, ℻ 505/989–5077. 5 suites. Outdoor hot tubs, spa. D, MC, V.*

Campgrounds

The Santa Fe National Forest is right in the city's backyard and includes the Dome Wilderness (5,200 acres in the volcanically formed Jemez Mountains) and the Pecos Wilderness (223,333 acres of high mountains, forests, and meadows at the southern end of the Rocky Mountain chain). Public campsites are open from May to October.

For specifics, call the **Santa Fe National Forest Office** (✉ 1220 S. St. Francis Dr., Box 1689, 87504, ☎ 505/988–6940). Some private campground operators provide literature at the **La Bajada Welcome Center** (✉ La Bajada Hill, 13 mi southwest of Santa Fe on I–25, ☎ 505/471–5242).

⚠ **Babbitt's Los Campos RV Resort.** The only full-service RV park within the city limits, Los Campos even has a swimming pool. Behind a car dealership on one side, the resort has open vistas on the other: poplars and Russian olive trees, a dry riverbed, and mountains rising in the background. ⊠ *3574 Cerrillos Rd., 87505,* ☎ *505/473–1949. 94 RV sites.* ⌨ *$23. Rest rooms, showers, LP gas, pool, picnic tables.*

⚠ **Rancheros de Santa Fe Campground.** This camping park is on a hill in the midst of a piñon forest. ⊠ *On I–25N, Old Las Vegas Hwy., 87505 (Exit 290 on the Las Vegas Hwy., 10½ mi from the Santa Fe Plaza),* ☎ *505/466–3482. 95 RV sites, 37 tent sites. Rest rooms, hot showers, LP gas, grocery, ice, pool, coin laundry.* ⌨ *Tent sites $16.95, water and electric hookups $20.95, full hookups $22.95–$23.95, cabins $29.95.*

⚠ **Santa Fe KOA.** In the foothills of the Sangre de Cristo Mountains, 20 minutes southeast of Santa Fe, this large campground is covered with piñons, cedars, and junipers. ⊠ *Old Las Vegas Hwy. (NM 3), Box 95-A, 87505,* ☎ *505/466–1419. 44 RV sites, 26 tent sites, 10 cabins. Rest rooms, hot showers, LP gas, grocery, recreation room, coin laundry.* ⌨ *Tent sites $17.95, water and electric hookups $20.95, full hookups $23.95, cabins $29.95.*

⚠ **Tesuque Pueblo RV Campground.** Operated by the Tesuque Pueblo, this campground is on an open hill with a few cedar trees dotting the landscape; off to the west is the Tesuque River. ⊠ *Box 360-H, Tesuque 87501 (10 mi north of Santa Fe; take I–25's St. Francis Exit),* ☎ *505/455–2661. 68 RV sites, 26 tent sites. Rest rooms, showers, drinking water, security gate, coin laundry.* ⌨ *Call for rates.*

NIGHTLIFE AND THE ARTS

Santa Fe is perhaps America's most cultured small city. Gallery openings, poetry readings, plays, and dance concerts take place year-round, not to mention the famed opera and chamber-music festivals. Check the arts and entertainment listings in Santa Fe's daily newspaper, the *New Mexican,* or the weekly *Santa Fe Reporter* for shows and events. Activities peak in the summer.

Nightlife

A handful of bars have spirited entertainment, from flamenco dancing to smokin' bands. Austin-based blues and country groups and other acts wander into town on occasion, but on most nights your best bet might be quiet cocktails beside the flickering embers of a piñon fire. Mellow entertainers perform nightly in many hotel bars.

Catamount Bar (⊠ 125 E. Water St., ☎ 505/988–7222) is popular with the post-college set; jazz and blues/rock groups play on weekends and some weeknights. **Club Alegría** (⊠ Agua Fria Rd. near Siler, ☎ 505/471–2324) is the venue for Friday-night salsa dance parties. **Dragon Room** (⊠ 406 Old Santa Fe Trail, ☎ 505/983–7712) at the Pink Adobe restaurant has been the place to see and be seen in Santa Fe for decades; flamenco and other light musical fare entertains patrons at the packed bar. **El Farol** (⊠ 808 Canyon Rd., ☎ 505/983–9912) is where locals like to hang out and listen to flamenco, country, folk, and blues; it's packed on weekend nights in summer. **Evangelo's** (⊠ 200 W. San Francisco St., ☎ 505/982–9014) has pool tables in a smoky basement, 200 types of imported beer, and rock bands on many weekends. **Rodeo Nites** (⊠ 2911 Cerrillos Rd., ☎ 505/473–4138) attracts a country-western crowd.

The Arts

Music

The acclaimed **Santa Fe Chamber Music Festival** (⊠ Museum of New Mexico in the Palace of the Governors, 113 Lincoln Ave., 87501, ☎ 505/983–2075) takes place in July and August at the St. Francis Auditorium.

Artistically and visually the city's crowning glory, the **Santa Fe Opera** (☎ 505/986–5900) performs in a strikingly modern structure—a 2,126-seat, indoor-outdoor amphitheater with excellent acoustics and sight lines. Carved into the natural curves of a hillside 7 mi north of the city on U.S. 84/285, the opera overlooks mountains, mesas, and sky. Add some of the most acclaimed singers, directors, conductors, musicians, designers, and composers from Europe and the United States, and you begin to understand the excitement that builds every June. Founded in 1956 by John Crosby, who remains its general director, the company presents five works in repertory each summer—a blend of seasoned classics, neglected masterpieces, and world premieres. Many evenings sell out far in advance, but inexpensive standing-room tickets are often available on the day of the performance.

Orchestral and chamber concerts are given at varying venues by the **Santa Fe Pro Musica** (☎ 505/988–4640) from September to May. Baroque and other classical compositions are the normal fare; the annual Christmas and Holy Week performances are highlights. **Santa Fe Summerscene** (☎ 505/438–8834) presents free concerts (rhythm and blues, light opera, jazz, Cajun, salsa, folk, and bluegrass), and dance performances (modern, folk) in the Santa Fe Plaza every Tuesday and Thursday from mid-June to August at noon and 6 PM. The **Santa Fe Symphony** (☎ 505/983–3530) performs seven concerts each season (from September to May) to sold-out houses at Sweeney Center (✉ 201 W. Marcy St.).

Theater

The **Greer Garson Theater** (✉ College of Santa Fe, 1600 St. Michael's Dr., ☎ 505/473–6511) stages comedies, dramas, and musicals from October to May. The **Santa Fe Community Theater** (✉ 142 East De Vargas St., ☎ 505/988–4262) has been presenting an adventurous mix of avant-garde pieces, classical drama, melodrama, and musical comedy since it was founded in 1922. The **Children's Theater** (☎ 505/984–3055) performs at the Santa Fe Community Theater year-round. **Santa Fe Stages** (☎ 505/982–6683), an international theater festival, is held from June to August at the Greer Garson Theater (☞ *above*) and includes dance performances and classical and contemporary productions. On Friday, Saturday, and Sunday during July and August, **Shakespeare in Santa Fe** (☎ 505/982–2910) presents performances of the Bard's finest in the courtyard of the John Gaw Meem Library at St. John's College (✉ 1160 Camino Cruz Blanca). Renaissance violin–hammer dulcimer music begins at 6, followed by the play at 7. Bring a picnic basket or buy food at the concession stand. Seating is limited to 350, so it's best to get tickets in advance. Tickets cost between $7 and $25. Grass and courtyard spots are free, though a $5 donation is suggested.

OUTDOOR ACTIVITIES AND SPORTS

On a shelf between the southernmost range of the Rocky Mountains, the Sangre de Cristos, and the high desert of north-central New Mexico, Santa Fe is a great place for outdoor activities. Head to the mountains for fishing, camping, and skiing; to the nearby Rio Grande for kayaking; and almost anywhere in the area for bird-watching and biking.

Participant Sports

Bicycling

A map of suggested bike trips—among them a 30-mi round-trip ride from downtown Santa Fe to the Santa Fe Ski Area—can be picked up at the **Convention and Visitors Bureau** (⊠ 201 W. Marcy St., ☎ 505/984–6760). **Palace Bike Rentals** (⊠ 409 E. Palace Ave., ☎ 505/986–0455) is a reliable and centrally located operation.

Bird-Watching

At the end of Upper Canyon Road alongside the Santa Fe River is the **Randall Davey Audubon Center,** a 135-acre nature sanctuary that harbors diverse birds and other wildlife. The site was once the home and studio of Randall Davey, a prolific early Santa Fe artist. Between June and August on weekends there are educational programs and free bird walks, and one afternoon a week at this time you can visit the Davey house (the day varies from year to year). ⊠ *Upper Canyon Rd.,* ☎ *505/983–4609.* ☎ *$1; house tour $3.* ☉ *Daily 9–5 for self-guided tours.*

Golf

The 18-hole, par-72 **Pueblo de Cochiti Golf Course** (⊠ 5200 Cochiti Hwy., Cochiti Lake, ☎ 505/465–2239), set against a backdrop of steep canyons and red-rock mesas, is a 45-minute drive southwest of the city. Cochiti, one of the top public golf courses in the country, has a greens fee of $25 on weekdays and $30 on weekends and holidays; an optional cart costs $10 per person. **Santa Fe Country Club** (⊠ Airport Rd., ☎ 505/471–0601), a tree-shaded semiprivate course, has driving and putting ranges and a pro shop. You can rent clubs and electric-carts.

Horseback Riding

New Mexico's rugged countryside has been the scene of many Hollywood westerns. Whether you want to ride the range that Kevin Costner and Gregory Peck rode or just head out feeling tall in the saddle, you can do so year-round. Rentals average about $20 an hour.

Bishop's Lodge (⊠ Bishop's Lodge Rd., ☎ 505/983–6377) provides rides and guides from April to November. **Galarosa Stable** (⊠ Galisteo, ☎ 505/983–6565 or 800/338–6877) provides rentals by the half day or full day south of Santa Fe in the panoramic Galisteo Basin. **Vientos Encantados** (⊠ Round Barn Stables, off U.S. 84/285, Ojo Caliente, ☎ 505/583–2233), a one-hour drive north of Santa Fe, conducts trail rides and pack trips near the Ojo Caliente mineral springs.

Jogging

Because of the city's altitude (7,000 ft), you may feel heavy-legged and light-headed if you start running shortly after you arrive. Once you've become acclimated, though, you'll find that this is a great place to run. There's a jogging path along the Santa Fe River, parallel to Alameda, and another at Fort Marcy on Washington Avenue. Every Wednesday evening the **Santa Fe Striders** (☎ 505/989–1819) organize a run from the Plaza.

Three races of note take place each year (☞ Santa Fe Convention and Visitors Bureau *in* Santa Fe A to Z, *below,* for more information): Runners turn out in droves on Labor Day for the **Old Santa Fe Trail Run.** The **Santa Fe Runaround,** a 10-km race held in early June, begins and ends at the Plaza. The **Women's Five-Kilometer Run** is held in early August.

Skiing

The **Santa Fe Ski Area,** usually open from Thanksgiving to Easter, is a fine if relatively small operation that receives an average of 250 inches of snow a year along with plenty of sunshine. One of America's highest ski areas—the summit is a little more than 12,000 ft above sea level—it has a variety of terrain and seems bigger than its 1,650 ft of vertical rise and 500 acres. There are some great powder stashes, tough bump runs, and many wide, gentle cruising runs. The 40-plus trails are ranked 20% beginner, 40% intermediate, and 40% advanced. The kids' center, Chipmunk Corner, provides day care for infants and supervised skiing for children. Rentals, a good cafeteria, a ski shop, and Totemoff's bar are other amenities. For information, call the Santa Fe Ski Area (☎ 505/982–4429) or Santa Fe Central Reservations (☎ 505/983–8200 or 800/776–7669 outside NM). For snow-condition information, call 505/983–9155.

For cross-country skiing conditions around Santa Fe, contact the **Santa Fe National Forest Office** (☎ 505/988–6940).

Tennis

Santa Fe has more than two dozen public tennis courts available on a first-come, first-served basis. For information about the public facilities listed below and additional ones, call the **City Parks Division** (☎ 505/473–7236).

There are four asphalt courts at **Alto Park** (⊠ 1035½ Alto St.), four concrete courts at **Herb Martínez/La Resolana Park** (⊠ Camino Carlos Rey), three asphalt courts at **Ortíz Park** (⊠ Camino de las Crucitas), and two asphalt courts at **Fort Marcy Complex** (⊠ Prince and Kearny Aves.).

Among the major private tennis facilities, including indoor, outdoor, and lighted courts, are **Club at El Gancho** (⊠ Old Las Vegas Hwy., ☎ 505/988–5000), **Sangre De Cristo Racquet Club** (⊠ 1755 Camino Corrales, ☎ 505/983–7978), **Santa Fe Country Club** (⊠ Airport Rd., ☎ 505/471–3378), and **Shellaberger Tennis Center** (⊠ College of Santa Fe, St. Michael's Dr., ☎ 505/473–6144).

Windsurfing

Strong summer breezes and a proximity to man-made lakes have made northern New Mexico a popular windsurfing spot, though the water can be chilly and the winds unpredictable. Early morning is the best time to go, because thunderstorms often occur in the afternoon. Devoted regulars head to **Abiquiú Lake,** (⊠ U.S. 84/285, Abiquiú, ☎ 505/685–4371), 40 mi northwest of Santa Fe; **Cochiti Lake** (⊠ I–25, Santo Domingo Exit, Peña Blanca, ☎ 505/242–8302), between Los Alamos and Santa Fe; and **Storrie Lake** (⊠ NM 518, off I–25, Las Vegas, ☎ 505/425–9231), 63 mi east of Santa Fe.

SHOPPING

Santa Fe has been a trading post for a long time. A thousand years ago the great pueblos of the Anasazi civilizations were strategically located between the buffalo-hunting tribes of the Great Plains and the Indians of Mexico. Native Americans in New Mexico traded turquoise, which was thought to have magical properties, and other valuables with Native Americans from Mexico for metals, shells, parrots, and other exotic items. After the arrival of the Spanish during the early 1600s and the subsequent development of the West in the early 1800s, Santa Fe became the place to exchange silver from Mexico and natural resources from New Mexico—including hides, fur, and foodstuffs—for manufactured goods, whiskey, and greenbacks from the United States. With the building of the railroad in 1880, all kinds of goods came and went through Santa Fe.

The trading legacy remains, but now downtown Santa Fe caters almost exclusively to tourists. Today's major commodity is the Santa Fe style, which is as distinctive as the city's architecture. The designs and materials and ethnic influences range from Native American to Hispanic to distant tribal cultures. No longer as hip as it was a few years ago, the style still has its admirers. There was a period when it had become such a cliché that a local produced a poster, "Another Victim of Santa Fe Style," that showed a Santa Fean lying faceup on a Native American rug, surrounded by howling-coyote carvings, a kiva fireplace, a beamed ceiling, a sun-bleached cattle skull, and a string of red chile peppers.

Santa Fe may seem like one big shopping mall, but a few retail areas stand out. Canyon Road is the most expensive. The downtown district, around the Plaza, contains shops, galleries, and restaurants. The Guadalupe neighborhood, which includes Sanbusco Center on the southwest perimeter of town, is a great place to window-shop and relax at a sidewalk café.

Art Galleries

Santa Fe's sparkling light, ancient cultures, and evocative landscape of mountains and mesas have long mesmerized

48

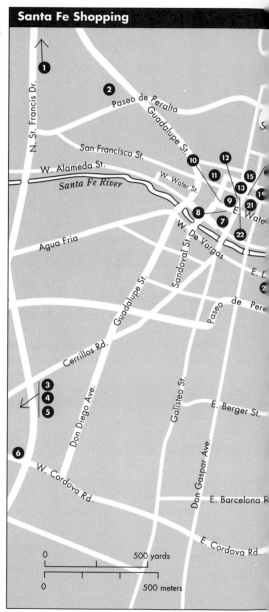

Santa Fe Shopping

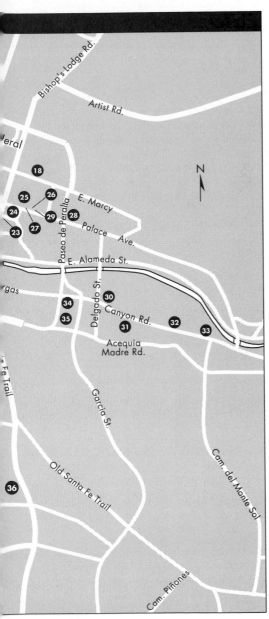

artists. "The world is wide here," said Georgia O'Keeffe, in her usual get-right-to-the-point manner. Santa Fe has emerged as a leading international center of contemporary and traditional Native American and Western art.

But before the arrival of such artists as Ernest L. Blumenschein and John Sloan in the early 20th century, an earlier form of art was popular in northern New Mexico. Bultos and retablos, both commonly known as santos, remain an indigenous, little-heralded art form. These devotional images have been part of everyday life in Mexico and the Southwest since Christianity arrived in the New World. No attempt has been made to mass-produce them, and no two are exactly alike. Tinwork, straw inlay, furniture-making, and weaving are other arts refined here by Hispanic artists through the centuries.

Santa Fe supports more than 100 art galleries. The following selection represents a good cross section; the Santa Fe Convention and Visitors Bureau (☞ Santa Fe A to Z, *below*) has a more extensive listing.

Andrew Smith Gallery (⊠ 203 W. San Francisco St., ☎ 505/984–1234) is a significant photo gallery dealing in works by Edward S. Curtis and other 19th-century chroniclers of the American West; major figures of the 20th century, including Ansel Adams, Eliot Porter, and Alfred Stieglitz; and regional artists including Barbara Van Cleve.

Bellas Artes (⊠ 653 Canyon Rd., ☎ 505/983–2745), a gallery and sculpture garden, carries contemporary pieces, pre-Columbian and African works, ceramics, and textiles.

Canyon Road Fine Art (⊠ 621 Canyon Rd., ☎ 505/988–9511) specializes in works by early Santa Fe artists and contemporary impressionist painters.

Charlotte Jackson Fine Art (⊠ 123 E. Marcy St., ☎ 505/989–8688) focuses on contemporary art dealing with light and space, including work by Joe Barnes, Anne Cooper, James Howell, and Roy Thurston.

Dewey Galleries (⊠ Catron Building, 53 Old Santa Fe Trail, ☎ 505/982–8632) shows historic Navajo textiles and jewelry, and paintings and sculptures.

Edith Lambert Galleries (✉ 300 Galisteo St., Suite 201, ☎ 505/984–2783 or 800/594–9667) represents some of the nation's most promising artists. Groundbreaking exhibits by metalsmiths, contemporary doll artists, and book artists are presented annually.

Gerald Peters Gallery (✉ 1011 Paseo de Peralta, ☎ 505/954–5700) is Santa Fe's leading gallery of 19th- and 20th-century American and European art. It has works by Charles M. Russell, Albert Bierdstadt, the Taos Society, the New Mexico Modernists, and Georgia O'Keeffe.

Leo Weaver Jewelry Galleries (✉ 137 W. Water St., ☎ 505/820–2110) displays high-quality works in contemporary and traditional designs by several dozen Taos artists. Check out the hand-stamped concha belts by silversmith Seth Brown and the imaginative jewelry by Anne Forbes.

Lew Allen and Lew Allen (✉ 129 W. Palace Ave., ☎ 505/988–8997) is a leading center for contemporary arts by internationally known and up-and-coming Southwest artists.

Nedra Matteucci Galleries (✉ 1075 Paseo de Peralta, ☎ 505/982–4631) exhibits works by California regionalists, members of the early Taos and Santa Fe schools, and masters of American Impressionism and Modernism. Spanish-colonial furniture, Indian antiquities, and a sculpture garden are other draws of this well-respected establishment.

New Millennium Fine Art (✉ 217 W. Water St., ☎ 505/983–2002) is a street-level showroom filled with contemporary Native American paintings and jewelry, signed posters and prints, contemporary landscapes, and photographs of Southwestern and Native American subjects.

Niman Fine Arts (✉ 125 Lincoln Ave., ☎ 505/988–5091) focuses on the prolific and outstanding work of two contemporary Native American artists—Hopi painter Dan Namingha and the late Apache sculptor Allan Houser.

Plan B Evolving Arts (✉ 1050 Old Pecos Trail, ☎ 505/982–1338), formerly the Center for Contemporary Art, is a showcase for up-and-coming young artists, with an emphasis on cutting-edge and avant-garde works. The adjacent Cinematheque screens foreign and independent films of the type that bypass mainstream theaters.

William R. Talbot Fine Art (⊠ 129 W. San Francisco St., ☎ 505/982–1559) sells antique maps and prints.

Wyeth Hurd Gallery (⊠ 301 E. Palace Ave., ☎ 505/989–8380) carries the work of the multigenerational arts family that includes N. C. Wyeth (who died in 1945); his children Andrew and Henriette Wyeth; Peter Hurd, Henriette's husband; Jamie Wyeth, Andrew's son; and Peter de la Fuente, Henriette and Peter's grandson.

Specialty Stores

Books

More than 20 stores in Santa Fe sell used books, and a handful of high-quality shops carry the latest releases from mainstream and small presses.

Collected Works Book Store (⊠ 208B W. San Francisco St., ☎ 505/988–4226) carries art and travel books, Southwestern titles, and paperbacks.

Nicholas Potter (⊠ 211 E. Palace Ave., ☎ 505/983–5434) specializes in used books, including some rare titles. The quixotic shop also stocks used jazz and classical CDs.

Clothing

Function dictates form in cowboy fashions. A wide-brimmed hat is essential in open country for protection from heat, rain, and insects. In the Southwest there's no such thing as a stingy brim. Cowboy hats made by Resistol, Stetson, Bailey, and other leading firms cost between $50 and $500, and hats made of fur and other exotic materials can fetch four figures. Small wonder that when it rains in Santa Fe or Albuquerque, some people are more concerned about protecting their hats than about getting wet.

Though they're now mostly fashion statements, some Western accessories were once merely functional. The pointed toes of cowboy boots slide easily in and out of stirrups, and high heels—worn for the same reason by Mongolian tribesmen—help keep feet in the stirrups. Tall tops protect ankles and legs on rides through brush and cactus country and can protect the wearer from a nasty shin bruise from a skittish horse.

A colorful bandanna protected an Old West cowboy from sunburn and windburn and served as a mask in windstorms, when riding drag behind a herd or, on occasions far rarer than Hollywood would have us believe, when robbing trains. A cowboy's vest enhanced his ability to maneuver during roping and riding chores and provided pocket space that his skintight pants—snug to prevent wrinkles in the saddle area—didn't. Belt buckles are probably the most sought-after accessories—gold ones go for as much as $1,000.

Jane Smith (⊠ 550 Canyon Rd., ☎ 505/988–4775) sells extraordinary handmade Western wear for women and men, from cowboy boots and sweaters to Plains Indians–styled beaded tunics.

Montecristi Custom Hat Works (⊠ 322 McKenzie St., ☎ 505/983–9598) is where the smart set goes for custom-made straw hats so snug they're all but guaranteed to stay on, even if you're driving in an open convertible.

Origins (⊠ 135 W. San Francisco St., ☎ 505/988–2323) is the town's oldest apparel and textile store, with an assortment of antique and folk costumes, as well as contemporary designs.

Santa Fe Boot Company (⊠ 950 W. Cordova Rd., ☎ 505/983–8415) stocks boots by all major manufacturers and more exotic styles designed by owner Marian Trujillo. Hats and Western outerwear are also sold.

Santa Fe Western Mercantile (⊠ 6820 Cerrillos Rd., ☎ 505/471–3655) carries a huge inventory of hats, boots, jeans, English and Western saddles, buckles, belts, and feed and health-care products for horses and livestock.

Western Warehouse (⊠ De Vargas Center, ☎ 505/982–3388; ⊠ Villa Linda Mall, ☎ 505/471–8775) sells all the top-name hats, boots, belts, and buckles.

Home Furnishings

Artesanos (⊠ 222 Galisteo St. and 1414 Maclovia St., ☎ 505/471–8020) is one of the best Mexican-import shops in the nation, with everything from leather chairs to papier-mâché *calaveras* (skeletons used in Day of the Dead celebrations), tinware, and Talavera tiles.

Dewey Trading Co. (✉ 53 Old Santa Fe Trail, ☎ 505/983–5855 or 800/444–9665) is the place to shop for Western blankets, including the largest Pendleton selection in the Southwest, and the Southwest Trail series by Hopi weaver Ramona Sakiestewa.

Foreign Traders (✉ 202 Galisteo St., ☎ 505/983–6441), a Santa Fe institution founded as the Old Mexico Shop in 1927 and still run by the same family, stocks handicrafts, antiques, and accessories from Mexico and other parts of the world.

Jackalope (✉ 2820 Cerrillos Rd., ☎ 505/471–8539) sprawls over 7 acres, incorporating several pottery barns, a furniture store, endless aisles of knickknacks from Latin America and Asia, and a huge greenhouse. There's a lunch counter, barnyard animals, and a prairie-dog village.

Montez Gallery (✉ Sena Plaza Courtyard, 125 E. Palace Ave., ☎ 505/982–1828) sells Hispanic works of religious art and decoration, including retablos, bultos, furniture, paintings, pottery, weavings, and jewelry.

Native American Arts and Crafts

Arrowsmith's (✉ 402 Old Santa Fe Trail, ☎ 505/989–7663) stocks eclectic crafts and cowboy-and-Indian artifacts. Prices run from a few dollars for arrowheads to $24,000 for a saddle embellished with 200 pounds of silver.

Cristof's (✉ 106 W. San Francisco St., ☎ 505/988–9881) has a large selection of pottery, sculpture, and contemporary Navajo weavings and sand paintings.

Joshua Baer & Co. (✉ 116½ E. Palace Ave., ☎ 505/988–8944) carries superb historic Navajo textiles and rare antique Pueblo weavings.

Morning Star Gallery (✉ 513 Canyon Rd., ☎ 505/982–8187) is a veritable museum of Native American art and artifacts. An adobe shaded by a huge cottonwood tree houses antique basketry, pre-1940 Navajo silver jewelry, Northwest coast Native American carvings, Navajo weavings, and art of the Plains Indians.

Packard's Indian Trading Co. (✉ 61 Old Santa Fe Trail, on the east side of the Plaza, ☎ 505/983–9241), the oldest Native American arts-and-crafts store on the Santa Fe Plaza, sells old pottery, saddles, and kachina dolls.

The Rainbow Man (✉ 107 E. Palace Ave., ☏ 505/982–8706), established in 1945, does business in the rebuilt remains of a building that was damaged during the 1680 Pueblo Revolt. The shop carries early Navajo, Mexican, and Chimayé textiles, plus photographs by Edward S. Curtis, jewelry, and miniature kachina dolls, some only an inch tall.

Trade Roots Collection (✉ 411 Paseo de Peralta, ☏ 505/982–8168) sells Native American ritual objects, such as fetish jewelry and Hopi rattles. The store is a good source of materials for craftspeople.

Flea Markets

Trader Jack's Flea Market (✉ U.S. 84/285, 7 mi north of Santa Fe), also known as the Santa Fe Flea Market, is considered the best flea market in America by its loyal legion of bargain hunters. The market is open from dawn to dusk from Friday to Sunday except between December and February (and sometimes even then if the weather's right). You can buy everything from a half-wolf puppy or African carvings to vintage cowboy boots, fossils, or a wall clock made out of an old hubcap. On 12 acres of land belonging to the Tesuque Pueblo, the market is right next to the Santa Fe Opera. ("There goes the neighborhood," quoth Trader Jack when the opera season starts.)

SIDE TRIPS

One can hardly grasp the profundity of New Mexico's ancient past or its immense landscape without journeying into the hinterlands. Each of the excursions below can be accomplished in a day or less.

Pecos National Historic Park

25 mi southeast of Santa Fe via I–25.

The centerpiece of Pecos National Historic Park is the **ruins of Pecos,** once a major Pueblo village. In a fertile valley between the Great Plains and the Rio Grande Valley, Pecos was a trading center centuries before the Spanish conquistadors visited in about 1540. The Spanish later returned to build two missions.

Containing more than 1,100 rooms in a structure as high as five stories, the pueblo once sheltered as many as 2,500 people. It was abandoned in 1838, and its 17 surviving occupants moved to the Jemez Pueblo. The ruins of the missions and of the excavated pueblo may be visited on a self-guided tour, which can be completed in about two hours. The pivotal Civil War Battle of Glorieta Pass took place on an outlying parcel of park land in late March 1862; its victory over Confederate forces firmly established the control of the Union army of the New Mexico Territory. At the park's entranceway is a visitor center. ⊠ *Pecos National Historic Park, Pecos,* ☎ *505/757–6414.* ☞ *$4 per car, $2 per tour-bus passenger.* ☉ *Memorial Day–Labor Day, weekdays 8–6; Labor Day–Memorial Day, weekdays 8–5.*

Jemez Country

In the Jemez region, the 1,000-year-old Anasazi ruins at the Bandelier National Monument present a vivid contrast to Los Alamos National Laboratory, birthplace of the atomic bomb. You can easily take in part of Jemez Country in a day trip from Santa Fe. On the loop described below you'll see terrific views of the Rio Grande Valley, the Sangre de Cristos, the Galisteo Basin, and, in the distance, the Sandias. The Anasazi ruins, in the canyons of the Pajarito Plateau, are striking as are the Bradbury Museum and Fuller Lodge in Los Alamos—for different reasons. A high-forest drive brings you to the awe-inspiring Valle Grande. There are places to eat and shop for essentials in Los Alamos and a few roadside diners in La Cueva, on the highway to Jemez Springs. To get oriented, stop at the **Los Alamos County Chamber of Commerce** (⊠ Fuller Lodge, 2132 Central Ave., Box 460 VG, Los Alamos 87544, ☎ 505/662–8105).

Los Alamos

31 mi from Santa Fe, north on U.S. 84/285 (to Pojoaque) and west on NM 502.

The town of Los Alamos, a 45-minute drive from Santa Fe, was founded in absolute secrecy in 1943 as a center of war research, and its existence only became known in 1945 with the detonation of atomic bombs in Japan. Los Alamos looks and feels utterly out of place in northern New Mexico, but it is a fascinating place to visit because of the profound role it played in shaping the modern world.

The **Bradbury Science Museum** is Los Alamos National Laboratory's public showcase. You can experiment with lasers; use advanced computers; witness research in solar, geothermal, fission, and fusion energy; and view exhibits about World War II's Project Y (the Manhattan Project, whose participants developed the atomic bomb). ⊠ *Los Alamos National Laboratory, 15th St. and Central Ave.,* ☎ *505/ 667–4444.* ⊡ *Free.* ◷ *Tues.–Fri. 9–5, Sat.–Mon. 1–5.*

The New Mexican architect John Gaw Meem designed the **Fuller Lodge,** a short drive up Central Avenue from the science museum. The massive log building was erected in 1928 as a dining and recreation hall for the small private boys' school that occupied this site. In 1942 the school was purchased by the federal government to serve as the base of operations for the Manhattan Project. Part of the lodge is an art center that shows the works of northern New Mexican artists and hosts temporary exhibits. ⊠ *2132 Central Ave.,* ☎ *505/662–9331.* ⊡ *Free.* ◷ *Mon.–Sat. 10–4.*

The **Los Alamos Historical Museum,** in a log building adjoining Fuller Lodge (☞ *above*), displays artifacts of early Native American life. Photographs and documents relate the community's history. ⊠ *2132 Central Ave.,* ☎ *505/662– 4493.* ⊡ *Free.* ◷ *Oct.–Apr., Mon.–Sat. 10–4 and Sun. 1–4; May–Sept., Mon.–Sat. 9:30–4:30 and Sun. 11–5.*

DINING AND LODGING

$–$$ ✕ **Hill Diner.** With a friendly staff and clientele, this large diner serves some of the finest burgers in town, along with chicken-fried steaks, homemade soups, and heaps of fresh vegetables. ⊠ *1315 Trinity Dr.,* ☎ *505/662–9745. AE, D, DC, MC, V.*

$$ ✕⛼ **Los Alamos Inn.** Rooms in this ground-level hotel have modern Southwestern decor and sweeping canyon views. Ashley's, the inn's restaurant and bar, serves American and

Southwestern regional specialties; the Sunday brunch is popular. ⊠ *2201 Trinity Dr., 87544,* ☎ ℻ *505/662–7211. 115 rooms. Restaurant, bar, pool. AE, D, DC, MC, V.*

$$ 🏨 **Hilltop House Hotel.** Minutes from the Los Alamos National Laboratory, this hotel hosts vacationers and scientists. All the rooms are furnished in modern Southwestern style; deluxe ones have kitchenettes. American and Southwestern cuisine is served at the restaurant, which has fabulous views of the Sangre de Cristos. ⊠ *400 Trinity Dr., at Central Ave. (Box 250), 87544,* ☎ *505/662–2441,* ℻ *505/662–5913. 87 rooms, 13 suites. Restaurant, lounge, indoor pool, exercise room, coin laundry. Continental breakfast. AE, D, DC, MC, V.*

$–$$ 🏨 **Orange Street Inn.** In an unremarkable 1948 wood-frame house in a quiet residential neighborhood, this B&B has rooms furnished in Southwestern and contemporary style. The public area has cable TV and a VCR, and you can use the kitchen and the laundry. ⊠ *3496 Orange St., 87544,* ☎ ℻ *505/662–2651. 8 rooms, 4 with bath. Continental breakfast. AE, D, DC, MC, V.*

Bandelier National Monument

40 mi from Santa Fe, north on U.S. 84/285, west on NM 502, south on NM 501 (W. Jemez Rd.) to "T" intersection with NM 4; turn left (east) and drive 6 mi to the monument's entrance.

Seven centuries before the Declaration of Independence was signed, compact city-states existed in the Southwest. Remnants of one of the most impressive can be seen at Frijoles Canyon in Bandelier National Monument. At the canyon's base, beside a gurgling stream, are the remains of cave dwellings, ancient ceremonial kivas, and other stone structures that stretch out for more than a mile beneath the sheer walls of the canyon's tree-fringed rim. For hundreds of years the Anasazi people, relatives of today's Rio Grande Pueblo Indians, thrived on wild game, corn, and beans. Suddenly, for reasons still undetermined, the settlements were abandoned. Climatic changes? A great drought? Crop failures? No one knows what caused the hasty retreat.

You may ponder these and other mysteries while following a paved, self-guided trail through the site. If you can climb primitive wooden ladders and squeeze through narrow doorways, you can explore some of the cave dwellings and get a feel for what it was like to live in the cell-like rooms.

Bandelier National Monument, named after author and ethnologist Adolph Bandelier (his novel, *The Delight Makers,* is set in Frijoles Canyon), contains 23,000 acres of backcountry wilderness, waterfalls, and wildlife. Sixty miles of trails traverse the park. A small museum in the visitor center focuses on the area's prehistoric and contemporary Native American cultures, with displays of artifacts from 1200 to modern times. ⊠ *Bandelier National Monument,* ☎ *505/ 672–3861.* ⌨ *$10 per car, good for 7 days.* ☉ *Memorial Day–Labor Day, daily 8–6; Labor Day–Memorial Day, daily 8–5.*

Valle Grande

40 mi west of Santa Fe. From Bandelier National Monument, head west (take a left) on NM 4 and follow the winding road through the mountain forest.

Valle Grande is one of the world's largest calderas. You can't imagine its immensity until you spot what look like specks of dust on the crater's lush meadow floor and realize they're cows. The entire 50-mi Jemez range, formed by cataclysmic upheavals, is filled with streams, hiking trails, campgrounds, and hot springs—reminders of its volcanic origin. If you're coming from Bandelier National Monument (☞ *above*), the drive should take about 45 minutes. It's particularly pretty in late September or early October when the aspens turn gold.

The High Road to Taos

If you are driving from Santa Fe to Taos and have a few extra hours, skip the main highway (NM 68) and take the far more scenic route, the High Road to Taos: U.S. 285 north to NM 503 northeast to NM 76 northeast to NM 75 east to NM 518 north. The drive through the rolling foothills and tiny valleys of the Sangre de Cristos, dotted with orchards, pueblos, and picturesque villages inhabited by weavers and wood carvers, is stunning. The high-road country is alluring in winter—when the fields are covered with quilts of snow, which trace the lines of homes, fences, and trees like bold pen-and-ink drawings against the sky—

but the roads can be icy and treacherous. Check on weather conditions before beginning the drive, or stay with the more conventional route. If you do decide to take the high road, you might want to save it for the return journey— the scenery is best enjoyed traveling north to south.

Nambé Pueblo

Head north from Santa Fe past Tesuque on U.S. 84/285; about 12 mi out of town at Pojoaque turn northeast (right) onto NM 503. Nambé Pueblo is off NM 503 about 4 mi down a side road.

At the Nambé Pueblo crafts center, near the Plaza and governor's office, you can purchase gold-flecked micaceous pottery, woven belts, and jewelry. There's a picnic area at the base of Nambé Falls and a large fishing lake that's open from March to November. The pueblo's main public ceremonial days are July 4 and October 4, the feast day of St. Francis. ⊠ *Nambé Pueblo Rd. off NM 503,* ☎ *505/455– 2036.*

Chimayó

25 mi north of Santa Fe. From Nambé Pueblo, return to NM 503; then continue to Chimayó.

Nestled into hillsides where gnarled piñons seem to grow from bare bedrock, Chimayó is famed for its weavings, its food, and its church.

Once you reach the village, you can't miss the signs for the **Santuario de Chimayó.** This small frontier adobe church has a fantastically carved, painted wood altar and is built on the site where, believers say, a mysterious light came from the ground on Good Friday in 1810. When people from the village investigated the phenomenon, the story goes, they pushed away the earth and found a large wooden crucifix. Today the chapel sits above a sacred *pozito* (a small hole), the dirt from which is believed to have miraculous healing properties, as the dozens of abandoned crutches and braces placed at the altar—along with many notes, letters, and photos left behind—dramatically testify. The Santuario draws a steady stream of worshipers all year long—Chimayó's nickname is "the Lourdes of the Southwest." During Holy Week as many as 50,000 people visit. The shrine is a National Historic Landmark, but unlike similar holy places, the commercialism here is limited to a small adobe shop nearby that sells brochures, books, and religious articles. ☎ *505/351–4889.* ⛱ *Free.* ☉ *Daily 9–5:30.*

DINING AND LODGING

$$–$$$ ✕ **Rancho de Chimayó.** In a century-old adobe hacienda tucked into the mountains, with whitewashed walls and hand-stripped vigas, cozy dining rooms, and lush, terraced patios, the Rancho de Chimayó is still owned and operated by the family that first occupied the house. There's a roaring fireplace in winter and, in summer, alfresco dining. ⊠ *NM 520,* ☎ *505/351–4444. Reservations essential. AE, MC, V.*

$ ✕ **Leona's de Chimayó.** This fast-food-style burrito and chile stand at one end of the Santuario de Chimayó parking lot has only a few tables, and in summer it's crowded. The specialty is flavored tortillas—everything from jalapeño to butterscotch. (Her business became so successful that owner Leona Tiede opened a tortilla factory in Chimayó's Manzana Center.) ⊠ *Off NM 503,* ☎ *505/351–4569. No credit cards.*

$$–$$$ 🏨 **Casa Escondida.** Intimate and serene, this adobe inn has sweeping views of the Sangre de Cristo range; the setting makes it a great base for mountain bikers. Chopin on the CD player and the scent of fresh-baked strudel waft through the rooms; owner Irenka Taurek, who speaks several languages, and manager Matthew Higgi provide an international welcome. Rooms are decorated with antiques and Native American and other regional arts and crafts. Ask for the Sun Room, in the main house, which has a private patio, viga ceilings, and a brick floor. The separate one-bedroom Casita Escondida has a kiva-style fireplace, tile floors, and a sitting area. A large hot tub is hidden in a grove behind wild berry bushes. ⊠ *Off NM 76 at Mile Marker 0100 (Box 142), 85722,* ☎ *505/351–4805 or 800/643–7201,* 🖷 *505/351–2575. 7 rooms, 1-bedroom house with full kitchen. Outdoor hot tub. Full breakfast. AE, MC, V.*

$$ 🏨 **Hacienda de Chimayó.** Rooms at this hotel are decorated with antiques, and each has a private bath and a fireplace. The mountain setting and the furnishings make this a choice accommodation. ⊠ *NM 520, 87522,* ☎ *505/351–2222. Continental breakfast. 6 rooms, 1 suite. AE, MC, V.*

\$\$ 🏠 **La Posada de Chimayó.** New Mexico's first B&B is a peaceful place whose two suites have fireplaces, Mexican rugs, handwoven bedspreads, and comfortable regional furniture. The entire guest house can be rented by the week. ⊠ *279 Rio Arriba, County Rd. 0101 (Box 463), 87522,* ☎ 𝔽𝔸𝕏 *505/351–4605. 2 suites. Full breakfast. No credit cards; 2–3 day minimum stay.*

SHOPPING

Ortega's Weaving Shop (⊠ NM 76 at County Rd. 98, ☎ 505/351–4215) sells Rio Grande–style textiles by the family whose Spanish ancestors brought the craft to New Mexico in the 1600s. The Galeria Ortega, next door, sells traditional New Mexican and Hispanic and contemporary Native American arts and crafts. The shop is closed on Sunday.

Truchas

35 mi north of Santa Fe; from Cordova, take NM 76 1½ mi north.

Truchas (Spanish for "trout") is where Robert Redford shot the movie *The Milagro Beanfield War* (based on a novel written by Taos author John Nichols). This breathtaking village is perched on the rim of a deep canyon beneath the towering Truchas Peaks, mountains high enough to be almost perpetually capped with snow. The tallest of the Truchas Peaks is 13,102 ft, the second-highest point in New Mexico.

SHOPPING

The most notable of the colorful shops and galleries in Truchas is **Cordova's Weaving Shop** (⊠ Box 425, ☎ 505/689–2437). The son of proprietor Harry Cordova acted in *The Milagro Beanfield War,* and the shop's back door made it into the film as the front door of the town's newspaper office.

Pueblos near Santa Fe

This trip will take you to several of the state's 19 pueblos, including San Ildefonso, one of the state's most picturesque, and Santa Clara, whose lands harbor a dramatic set of ancient cliff dwellings. Plan on spending about two hours at each pueblo.

Pojoaque Pueblo

12 mi north of Santa Fe on U.S. 84/285.

There is not much to see in the pueblo's plaza area, which hardly has a visible core, but the state visitor center and adjoining **Poeh Cultural Center and Museum** on U.S. 84/285 are worth a visit. The latter is an impressive complex of traditional adobe buildings, including the three-story Sun Tower, which contains a museum, a cultural center, and artists' studios. There are frequent demonstrations by artists, exhibitions, and, in warm weather, traditional ceremonial dances. By the early 20th century the pueblo was virtually uninhabited, but the survivors eventually began to restore it. Pojoaque's feast day is celebrated with dancing on December 12. Sketching, photography, and video cameras are not allowed at the pueblo. ⊠ *Rte. 11,* ☎ *505/455–2278.* ✆ *Free.* ☉ *Daily 8–5.*

San Ildefonso Pueblo

19 mi north of Santa Fe on U.S. 84/285. From the Pojoaque Pueblo, return to U.S. 84/285, but exit almost immediately onto NM 502 toward Los Alamos. Continue for about 7 mi until you reach the turnoff for San Ildefonso.

Maria Martinez, one of the most famous Pueblo potters in the world, lived here. She first created her exquisite "black on black" pottery in 1919 and in doing so sparked a major revival of all Pueblo arts and crafts. Though she died in 1980, the 26,000-acre San Ildefonso Pueblo remains a major center for pottery making and other arts and crafts. Many artists sell from their homes, and there are trading posts, a visitor center, and a museum where some of Martinez's work can be seen on weekdays. San Ildefonso is also one of the more visually appealing pueblos, with a well-defined plaza core and a spectacular setting beneath the Pajarito Plateau and Black Mesa. The pueblo's feast day is January 23, when unforgettable Buffalo, Deer, and Comanche dances are performed from dawn to dusk. Cameras are not permitted at any of the ceremonial dances but may be used at other times with a permit. ⊠ *NM 5,* ☎ *505/455–3549.* ✆ *$3 per car; $5 for still cameras, $25 for video recorders, and $15 for sketching.* ☉ *Daily 8–5.*

Ojo Caliente

55 mi north of Santa Fe on U.S. 285.

Ojo Caliente is home to natural hot springs at the only place in North America where five different types of mineral waters—iron, lithia, arsenic, salt, and soda—converge. The town was named by Spanish explorer Cabeza de Vaca, who visited in 1535 and believed he had stumbled upon the Fountain of Youth. He recorded his excitement in his journal:

"The greatest treasure I have found these strange people to possess are some hot springs which burst out of the foot of a mountain that gives evidence of being an active volcano. So powerful are the chemicals contained in this water that the inhabitants have a belief that the waters were given to them by their gods after weeping many tears. From the effect of the waters upon my remaining men, I am inclined to believe that the waters will do many things that our doctors are not capable of doing . . . I believe I have found the Fountain of Youth."

Modern-day visitors draw similar conclusions about the restorative powers of the springs, and they find that little has changed through the centuries. The spa itself, built in the 1920s (no one knows the exact date), is a no-frills establishment that includes a hotel and cottages (☞ *below*), a restaurant, a gift shop, massage rooms, men's and women's bathhouses, a chlorine-free swimming pool, and indoor and outdoor mineral tubs. The hotel, one of the original bathhouses, and the springs are all on the National Register of Historic Places, as is the adjacent Round Barn, from which visitors can take horseback tours and guided hikes to the ruins of ancient pueblo dwellings and petroglyph-etched rocks. Spa services include wraps, massage, and acupuncture. The setting at the foot of sandstone cliffs, atop which sit the ruins of ancient Indian pueblos, is nothing short of inspiring.

$$$ 🏨 **Ojo Caliente Mineral Springs Spa and Resort.** Accommodations at this spa are decidedly spartan but clean and comfortable, with down comforters on the beds and rudimentary bathrooms without showers or tubs—you've come for the mineral springs, after all (the bathhouse is equipped with showers). The lodgings have no phones, but bathrobes and the morning newspaper are supplied. Some of the cottages have kitchenettes. ⊠ *50 Los Banos Dr., off U.S. 285, 30 mi north of Española (Box 68), 87549,* ☎ *505/583–2233 or 800/222–9162,* FAX *505/583–2464. 19 rooms, 19 cottages. AE, D, DC, MC, V.*

Santa Clara Pueblo

27 mi northwest of Santa Fe. From San Ildefonso Pueblo, return to NM 502 and continue west across the Rio Grande to NM 30. Turn north (right) and continue 6 mi to the turnoff to the Puyé Cliff Dwellings. Proceed on this gravel road 9 mi to Santa Clara Pueblo.

Santa Clara Pueblo, southwest of Española, is the home of a historic treasure—the awesome **Puyé Cliff Dwellings,** which are in a canyon 9 mi up a gravel road south of the village off NM 503. The pueblo also contains four ponds, miles of stream fishing, picnicking, and camping facilities. You can tour the cliff dwellings, which are topped by the ruins of a 740-room pueblo, on your own or with a guide. Permits for the use of trails, camping, and picnic areas, as well as for fishing in trout ponds, are available at the sites. Shops in the village sell burnished red pottery, engraved blackware, paintings, and other arts and crafts. The pueblo's feast day of St. Clare is celebrated on August 12. ⊠ *Off NM 503, Española,* ☎ *505/753–7326.* ☞ *Pueblo free, cliff dwellings $5, video and still cameras $5.* ⊙ *Daily 8–4:30.*

SANTA FE A TO Z

Arriving and Departing

By Bus

Texas, New Mexico & Oklahoma Coaches (⊠ 858 St. Michael's Dr., ☎ 800/231–2222), which is affiliated with Greyhound, serves Santa Fe.

The **bus station** (⊠ 858 St. Michael's Dr., ☎ 505/471–0008) is south of downtown.

By Car

Interstate 25 passes east–west through Santa Fe, which is 58 mi northeast of Albuquerque. U.S. 84/285 runs north–south through the city.

By Plane
See Air Travel *in* Essential Information.

By Train
Amtrak (☎ 800/872–7245) operates the *Southwest Chief* between Chicago and Los Angeles. The train stops in Lamy, 18 mi south of Santa Fe.

You need to reserve a day ahead for the **shuttle bus** (☎ 505/982–8829) to and from Santa Fe. The cost each way is $14.

Getting Around

The majority of museums, galleries, shops, and restaurants in downtown Santa Fe are in walking distance of the Plaza. You need to take a car or a bus to get to the city's outer reaches, including the Museum of International Folk Art and the Museum of Indian Arts and Culture.

By Bus
The city's bus system, **Santa Fe Trails** (☎ 505/438–1464), covers six major routes: Agua Fria, Cerrillos, West Alameda, Southside, Eastside, and Galisteo. A daily pass costs $1. Buses run about every 30 minutes on weekdays, every hour on weekends. Service begins at 6 AM and continues until 10 PM on weekdays and until 8 PM on Saturday. There is no bus service on Sunday.

By Car
For car rental companies in Santa Fe, *see* Car Rental *in* Essential Information. Parking in Santa Fe is difficult, but public and private lots can be found throughout the city.

By Taxi
Capital City Cab Company (☎ 505/438–0000) controls all the cabs in Santa Fe. The taxis aren't metered; you pay a flat fee determined by the distance you're traveling. There are no cab stands; you must phone to arrange a ride. Trips within the city cost between $4 and $7. You can pick up a 40% taxi discount coupon at the Santa Fe Public Library (☞ Visitor Information, *below*).

Guided Tours

General-Interest

Aboot About (☎ 505/988–2774) leads walking tours that survey the history, art, and architecture of Santa Fe. Tours ($10) leave daily at 9:30 and 1:30 from the Eldorado Hotel and at 9:45 and 1:45 from the Hotel St. Francis. **Afoot in Santa Fe Walking Tours** (✉ 211 Old Santa Fe Trail, ☎ 505/983–3701) conducts a 2½-hour close-up look at the city. The tours ($10) leave from the Inn at Loretto from Monday to Saturday at 9:30 and 1:30 and on Sunday at 9:30. **Discover Santa Fe** (✉ 508 W. Cordova, ☎ 505/982–4979) tailors tours and itineraries for individuals, families, and groups. **Gray Line Tours of Santa Fe** (✉ 1330 Hickox St., ☎ 505/983–9491) operates guided outings to Taos, the Bandelier Cliff Dwellings, Los Alamos, and the Santa Clara Pueblo.

Special-Interest

The **Santa Fe Botanical Garden** (☎ 505/438–1684) schedules walks and gardens tours from May to September. **Recursos** (✉ 826 Camino de Monte Rey, ☎ 505/982–9301) operates historical, cultural, and nature tours.

Contacts and Resources

Emergencies

Ambulance, Fire and **Police** (☎ 911). **Lovelace Urgent Care** (✉ 901 W. Alameda, ☎ 505/995–2500; ✉ 440 St. Michael's Dr., ☎ 505/995–2400). **Medical Emergency Room, St. Vincent Hospital** (✉ 455 St. Michael's Dr., ☎ 505/820–5250). **Medical Dental Center** (✉ 465 St. Michael's Dr., Suite 205, ☎ 505/983–8089).

24-Hour Pharmacy

Walgreens (✉ 1096 S. St. Francis Dr., ☎ 505/982–9811).

Visitor Information

Santa Fe Chamber of Commerce (✉ 510 N. Guadalupe St., Suite L, De Vargas Center N, 87504, ☎ 505/983–7317). **Santa Fe Convention and Visitors Bureau** (✉ 201 W. Marcy St., Box 909, 87504, ☎ 505/984–6760 or 800/777–2489). **Santa Fe Public Library** (✉ 145 Washington Ave., ☎ 505/984–6780).

3 Taos

In case you want to see the world.

In case you want to be welcomed there.

We're here to see that you're always welcomed at establishments everywhere. That's why millions of people carry the American Express® Card – for peace of mind, confidence, and security, around the world or just around the corner.

In case you're running low.

We're here to help with more than 118,000 Express Cash locations around the world. In order to enroll, just call American Express before you start your vacation.

do more

And just in case.

We're here with American Express® Travelers Cheques and Cheques *for Two*.® They're the safest way to carry money on your vacation and the surest way to get a refund, practically anywhere, anytime.
Another way we help you...

do more®

Travelers Cheques

TAOS CASTS A LINGERING SPELL on the memory. Stately elms and cottonwood trees frame sometimes narrow streets, and one- and two-story adobe buildings line the two-centuries-old Plaza. The adobes reveal the influence of Native American and Spanish settlers; rugged beams support the overhanging balconies added later by American pioneers who ventured west after the Mexican War of 1846. Some of the roads extending from the Plaza remain unpaved. When it rains, they're not unlike the rutted streets of yesteryear.

Updated by Nancy Zimmerman

With a population of about 6,500, Taos, on a rolling mesa at the base of the Sangre de Cristo Mountains, is actually three towns in one. The first is the business district of art galleries, restaurants, and shops that recalls the Santa Fe of a few decades ago. The second area, 3 mi north of the commercial center, is the Taos Pueblo, where Taos-Tiwa Native American people live. The third, 4 mi south of town, is Ranchos de Taos, a farming and ranching community settled centuries ago by the Spanish. Ranchos de Taos is best known for the San Francisco de Asís Church, whose buttressed adobe walls shelter significant religious artifacts and paintings. Its *camposanto* (graveyard) is one of the most photographed in the country.

Life at the Taos Pueblo predates Marco Polo's 13th-century travels in China and the arrival of the Spanish in America in the 1500s. Unlike many nomadic Native American tribes that were forced to relocate to government-designated reservations, the residents of Taos Pueblo have inhabited their land (at present 95,000 acres) at the base of the 12,282-ft-high Taos Mountain for centuries.

That so many 20th-century painters, photographers, and literary figures—among them Georgia O'Keeffe, Ansel Adams, and D. H. Lawrence—have been drawn to the earthy spirit of Taos has only heightened its appeal. Bert Geer Phillips and Ernest Leonard Blumenschein, traveling from Denver on a planned painting trip into Mexico in 1898, stopped in Taos to have a broken wagon wheel repaired. Enthralled with the landscape, earth-hued adobe buildings, piercing light, and clean mountain air, they discontinued their journey south. They returned to the Taos area often, speaking so highly of it that other East Coast artists followed them west. By 1915, the Taos Society of Artists had been established. Blumenschein and Phillips, with Joseph Henry Sharp and Eanger Irving Couse, all graduates of the Parisian art school Académie Julian, formed the core of the group.

Most of the early Taos artists spent their winters in New York or Chicago teaching painting or illustration to earn enough money to summer in New Mexico. Living conditions were primitive then: no running water, electricity, or even indoor plumbing. But these painters happily endured such inconveniences to indulge their fascination with Native American customs, modes of dress, and ceremonies. Eventually, they co-opted the Native architecture and dress and presumptuously fancied that they "knew" Indian culture. The society disbanded in 1927, but Taos continued to attract artists. Several galleries opened and, in 1952, local painters joined together to form the Taos Artists' Association, forerunner to today's Taos Art Association. At present, several dozen galleries and shops (☞ Shopping, *below*) display art, sculpture, and crafts.

EXPLORING TAOS

Taos is small and decidedly lacking in glamour, but this highly walkable community is a welcoming place to explore. You'll need a car to reach the Enchanted Circle, the Rio Grande Gorge, and other places of interest beyond Taos proper. A word of caution for drivers: Traffic can be heavy in the peak summer and winter seasons; be prepared for snarls.

The Kit Carson Historic Museums of Taos consortium includes the Blumenschein Home and the Kit Carson Home and Museum (☞ Sights to See *in* Taos Plaza and Bent Street, *below,* for both) and La Hacienda de Don Antonio Severino Martínez (☞ Sights to See *in* Ranchos de Taos and Points South, *below*). Each of the museums charges $5 admission, but at any of the participating facilities you can buy a joint ticket—$7.50 for two museums, $10 for all three.

Taos Plaza and Bent Street

More than four centuries after it was laid out, Taos Plaza remains the center of commercial life in Taos. Bent Street, where New Mexico's first American governor lived and died, is the town's upscale shopping area and gallery enclave.

Numbers in the text correspond to numbers in the margin and on the Exploring Taos map.

A Good Walk

Begin at the gazebo in the middle of **Taos Plaza** ①. After exploring the plaza, head south from its western edge down the small unmarked alley (its name is West Plaza Drive). The first intersection you reach is Camino de la Placita. Across Camino de la Placita, West Plaza Drive becomes Ledoux Street. Continue south on Ledoux to the **Blumenschein Home** ② and, a few doors farther south, the **Harwood Foundation** ③. (If you're driving, the parking area for the Harwood Foundation is at Ledoux and Ranchitos Road.)

Ranchitos Road is directly across Ledoux Street from the front door of the Harwood Foundation. Head back north on Ranchitos a few blocks, make a left on Camino de la Placita, walk a short way, make a right onto Don Fernando Road, and follow it east along the north side of the Plaza to Paseo del Pueblo Norte (NM 68), which is the main street of Taos. As you continue east across NM 68, the name of Don Fernando changes to Kit Carson Road. On the north side of Kit Carson Road is the **Kit Carson Home and Museum** ④. After visiting the home, head back to Paseo del Pueblo Norte and walk north past the Taos Inn to Bent Street (on your left), where you can browse through the boutiques and galleries.

In a tiny plaza is the **Governor Bent Museum** ⑤, the modest home of the first Anglo governor of the state. Across the street is the John Dunn House. Once the homestead of a notorious Taos gambler and transportation entrepreneur, the Dunn House is now a small shopping plaza (☞ Shopping, *below*). At the western edge of Bent Street, head north (to the right) on Camino de la Placita. In about 2½ blocks you'll come to the Taos Volunteer Fire Department building, which doubles as a fire station and the **Firehouse Collection** ⑥ exhibition space.

Civic Plaza Drive runs along the southern edge of the Fire Department building. Head east (to the left) on Civic Plaza and cross Paseo del Pueblo Norte. The **Stables Art Center** ⑦ will be to the south (the right) and **Kit Carson Memorial Park** ⑧ will be to the north. North of the park on Paseo del Pueblo Norte is the **Fechin Institute** ⑨, named for the iconoclastic artist Nicolai Fechin. On 10 handsome acres north of the Fechin Institute on Paseo del Pueblo Norte is the **Van Vechten–Lineberry Taos Art Museum** ⑩.

TIMING

The entire walk can be done in a half day, a whole day if you stop to lunch along the way and browse in the shops and galleries. The Fechin Institute is open between Memorial Day and October from Wednesday to Sunday, and by appointment only between November and Memorial Day. Some museums are closed on the weekend, so you may want to do this walk on a Wednesday, Thursday, or Friday. You'll be able to tour the museums in less than an hour each.

Sights to See

② **Blumenschein Home.** A visit to the residence of Ernest L. Blumenschein provides a glimpse into the cosmopolitan lives led by the members of the Taos Society of Artists, of which Blumenschein was a founding member. Most of the rooms in the adobe-style structure date from 1797. On display are the art, antiques, and other personal possessions of Blumenschein and his wife, Mary Greene Blumenschein, who along with their daughter Helen also painted. Several of Ernest Blumenschein's oil paintings hang in his former studio. ⊠ *222 Ledoux St.,* ☎ *505/758–0505.* ☑ *$5 (or use Kit Carson Historic Museums of Taos joint ticket;* ☞ *above).* ☉ *Daily 9–5.*

★ ⑨ **Fechin Institute.** The interior of this extraordinary adobe house, built between 1927 and 1933 by Russian émigré and artist Nicolai Fechin, is a marvel of carved Russian-style woodwork and furniture that glistens with an almost golden sheen. Fechin constructed it to showcase his daringly colorful portraits and landscapes. Fechin's daughter Eya oversees her father's architectural masterpiece—she loves talking about him and life "back then." Listed in the National Register of Historic Places, the Fechin Institute hosts exhibits

Exploring Taos

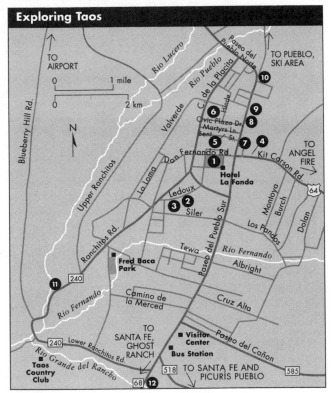

TO AIRPORT

TO PUEBLO, SKI AREA

Rio Lucero

Rio Pueblo

Paseo del Pueblo Norte

C. de la Placita

Hinde

0 1 mile
0 2 km

N

Blueberry Hill Rd.

Valverde

Civic Plaza Dr.
Martyrs Ln.
Bent   St.

Upper Ranchitos

La Loma

Don Fernando Rd.

Kit Carson Rd.

TO ANGEL FIRE

64

Hotel La Fonda

Ledoux

Siler

Montoya

Burch

Dolan

Ranchitos Rd.

Los Pandos

Fred Baca Park

240

Tewa

Paseo del Pueblo Sur

Rio Fernando

Albright

Rio Fernando

Camino de la Merced

Cruz Alta

TO SANTA FE, GHOST RANCH

Visitor Center

Bus Station

Paseo del Cañon

240 Lower Ranchitos Rd.

Rio Grande del Rancho

Taos Country Club

68 12

518 TO SANTA FE AND PICURIS PUEBLO

585

Blumenschein Home, **2**

Fechin Institute, **9**

Firehouse Collection, **6**

Governor Bent Museum, **5**

Harwood Foundation, **3**

Kit Carson Home and Museum, **4**

Kit Carson Memorial Park, **8**

La Hacienda de Don Antonio Severino Martínez, **11**

San Francisco de Asís Church, **12**

Stables Art Center, **7**

Taos Plaza, **1**

Van Vechten – Lineberry Taos Art Museum, **10**

and special workshops devoted to the artist's unique approach to learning, teaching, and creating. ✉ *227 Paseo del Pueblo Norte,* ☎ *505/758–1710.* 🖼 *$3.* ☉ *Memorial Day weekend–Oct., Wed.–Sun. 10–5, or by appointment.*

⑥ Firehouse Collection. More than 100 works by well-known Taos artists like Joseph Sharp, Ernest L. Blumenschein, and Bert Phillips hang in the Taos Volunteer Fire Department building. The exhibition space adjoins the station house, where five fire engines are maintained at the ready and an antique fire engine is on display. ✉ *323 Camino de la Placita,* ☎ *505/758–3386.* 🖼 *Free.* ☉ *Weekdays 8–4.*

⑤ Governor Bent Museum. In 1846, when New Mexico became a U.S. territory as a result of the Mexican War, Charles Bent, a trader, trapper, and mountain man, was appointed governor. A year later he was killed in his house by an angry mob protesting New Mexico's annexation by the United States. Governor Bent was married to María Ignacia, the older sister of Josefa Jaramillo, the wife of mountain man Kit Carson. The hoard of Western Americana and other memorabilia nearly overwhelms the adobe building where Bent lived. ✉ *117A Bent St.,* ☎ *505/758–2376.* 🖼 *$1.* ☉ *Daily 10–5.*

★ ③ Harwood Foundation. The Pueblo Revival former home of Burton C. Harwood, one of the original members of the Taos Society of Artists, is adjacent to a museum dedicated to the works of local artists. Taos Mountain looms in the background of *Winter Funeral* (circa 1932), a large landscape painting by Victor Higgins that hangs over a fireplace on the museum's first floor. Mabel Dodge Luhan, a major arts patron, bequeathed many of the 19th-century and early 20th-century works in the Harwood's collection, including *retablos* (painted wood representations of Catholic saints) and *bultos* (three-dimensional carvings of the saints). A new gallery with works by Agnes Martin was part of a recently completed expansion project at the museum, which is a department of the University of New Mexico. ✉ *238 Ledoux St.,* ☎ *505/758–9826.* 🖼 *$4.* ☉ *Tues.–Sat. 10–5, Sun. noon–5.*

④ Kit Carson Home and Museum. Kit Carson bought this low-slung 12-room adobe home in 1843 as a wedding gift for Josefa Jaramillo, the daughter of a powerful, politically influential Mexican family. Josefa was 14 when the dashing twice-married mountain man and scout began courting her. Three of the museum's rooms are furnished as they were when the Carson family lived here. The rest of the museum is devoted to gun and mountain-man exhibits, early Taos antiques, artifacts, and manuscripts. ⊠ *Kit Carson Rd.,* ☎ *505/758–4741.* 🎟 *$5 (or use Kit Carson Historic Museums of Taos joint ticket;* ☞ *above).* ☉ *Nov. 2–Mar., daily 9–5; Apr.–Nov. 1, daily 8–6.*

🖐 **⑧ Kit Carson Memorial Park.** The noted pioneer is buried in the park that bears his name. His grave is marked with a *cerquita* (a spiked wrought-iron rectangular fence), traditionally used to outline and protect burial sites. Also interred here is Mabel Dodge Luhan, the pioneering patron of the early Taos art scene, whose friends and acquaintances included Georgia O'Keeffe, Ansel Adams, Aldous Huxley, D. H. Lawrence, Martha Graham, and Carl Jung. In addition to supporting the arts, Luhan, who arrived in Taos in 1917, had hoped to foster a utopian world order based on her perceptions about life at Taos Pueblo. The 20-acre park has swings and slides for recreational breaks. It's well marked with big stone pillars and a gate. ⊠ *Paseo del Pueblo Norte at Civic Plaza Dr.,* ☎ *505/758–8234.* 🎟 *Free.* ☉ *Memorial Day–Labor Day, daily 8–8; Labor Day–Memorial Day, daily 8–5.*

❼ Stables Art Center. It was in the stables in back of this house that the Taos Artists' Association first began showing the works of member and invited nonmember artists from across northern New Mexico. In 1952 the association purchased the handsome adobe building, which is now the visual arts gallery of the Taos Art Association. All the work on exhibit is for sale. ⊠ *133 Paseo del Pueblo Norte,* ☎ *505/758–2036.* 🎟 *Free.* ☉ *Daily 10–5.*

❶ Taos Plaza. The first European explorers of the Taos Valley came here with Captain Hernando de Alvarado, a member of Francisco Vásquez de Coronado's Expedition of 1540. Basque explorer Don Juan de Oñate arrived in Taos in July 1598 and established a mission and trading arrangements with residents of Taos Pueblo. The settlement actually developed into two plazas: The Plaza at the heart of the town became a thriving business district for the early colony; a walled residential plaza was constructed a few hundred yards behind and remains active today, home to a throng of gift and coffee shops. As authorized by a special act of Congress, the U.S. flag flies in the center of the Plaza day and night in recognition of Kit Carson's heroic stand protecting it from Confederate sympathizers during the Civil War. Next to a covered gazebo, donated by heiress and longtime Taos resident Mabel Dodge Luhan, is the Tiovivo, an antique carousel that thrills children during the three-day-long Fiestas de Santiago y Santa Ana in July. Tickets are 50¢ per ride. On the southeastern corner of Taos Plaza is the Hotel La Fonda de Taos. Some infamous erotic paintings by D. H. Lawrence that were naughty in his day but are quite tame by present standards can be viewed ($2 entry fee) in the manager's office.

⑩ Van Vechten–Lineberry Taos Art Museum. This museum shows the works of painter Duane Van Vechten, the late wife of Edwin C. Lineberry. Her former studio is the entrance to the museum, whose collection of about 125 works by more than 50 Taos artists includes works by all of the founders of the Taos Society of Artists. ⊠ *501 Paseo del Norte,* ☎ *505/758–2690.* ⊡ *$5.* ☉ *Wed.–Fri. 11–4, weekends 1:30–4.*

Ranchos de Taos and Points South

Numbers in the text correspond to numbers in the margin and on the Exploring Taos map.

A Good Drive

Head south 3 mi on NM 240 (also known as Ranchitos Road) to **La Hacienda de Don Antonio Severino Martínez** ⑪. As you pass by the tiny adobe cottages dotting the landscape, you'll get a sense of an older way of life that mirrors what you'll see at the hacienda. From the hacienda follow Ranchitos Road (NM 240) south and east another 4 mi to NM 68 and the small farming village of **Ranchos de Taos.** Head south (to the right) on NM 68, and look for the signs for **San Francisco de Asís Church** ⑫, which is on the east side of NM 68 (your left as you're driving south).

The small plaza here contains several shops worth checking out. Two sites off the beaten path from Ranchos de Taos are **Picurís Pueblo** and **Ghost Ranch.**

TIMING

Set aside about two hours to tour the hacienda, a bit of Ranchos de Taos, and San Francisco de Asís Church. You'll need to make a day of this tour if you continue on to Picurís Pueblo or Ghost Ranch.

Sights to See

⓫ **La Hacienda de Don Antonio Severino Martínez.** Spare and fortlike, this adobe structure built between 1804 and 1827 on the banks of the Rio Pueblo served as a community refuge from Comanche and Apache raids. Its thick adobe walls, which have few windows, surround two central courtyards. Don Antonio Severino Martínez was a farmer and trader; the hacienda was the final stop along *El Camino Real* (the Royal Road), the trade route the Spanish established between Mexico City and New Mexico. The restored period rooms here contain textiles, foods, and crafts of the early 19th century. There's a working blacksmith's shop, and weavers create beautiful clothes on reconstructed period looms. During the last weekend in September the hacienda hosts the Old Taos Trade Fair, a reenactment of fall trading fairs of the 1820s, when Plains Indians and trappers came to Taos to trade with the Spanish and the Pueblo Indians. The two-day event includes crafts demonstrations, native foods, and entertainment. ⊠ *Ranchitos Rd. (NM 240)*, ☎ *505/758–1000.* ⌨ *$5 (or use Kit Carson Historic Museums of Taos joint ticket;* ☞ *above).* ☉ *Daily 9–5.*

OFF THE BEATEN PATH

PICURÍS PUEBLO – The Picurís (Keresan for "those who paint") Native Americans once lived in six- and seven-story dwellings similar to those still standing at the Taos Pueblo, but these were abandoned in the wake of 18th-century Pueblo uprisings. Relatively isolated about 40 mi south of Taos, Picurís, one of the smallest pueblos in New Mexico, is surrounded by the timberland of the Carson National Forest. The 270-member Tiwa-speaking Picurís tribe is a sovereign nation and has no treaties with any country, including the United States. You can tour the village and 700-year-old ruins of kivas and storage areas, which were excavated in

1961. The exhibits in the pueblo's museum include pottery and some ruins. A separate building contains a restaurant (renovations for which were scheduled to be completed by spring 1999) and the Picurís Market, a convenience store and crafts shop. Fishing, picnicking, and camping are allowed at nearby trout-stocked Pu-Na and Tu-Tah lakes. Fishing and camping permits can be obtained at the Picurís Market. The pueblo honors its patron saint, San Lorenzo, with a festival on August 9 and 10. ⊠ *NM 75 (from Ranchos de Taos head south on NM 518, east on NM 75, and turn right at signs for village; from NM 68 head east on NM 75 and make a left into the village), Peñasco,* ☎ *505/587–2957.* 🎫 *Museum and store free; self-guided walking or driving tours of village and ruins $1.75; still camera permit (includes the $1.75 fee for the person with the camera) $5; video-camera or sketching permit (includes $1.75 fee) $10.* ☉ *Daily 9–6, but call ahead especially Labor Day–Memorial Day, when the pueblo is sometimes closed.*

Ranchos de Taos. This Spanish-colonial ranching and farming community, an early home to Taos Native Americans, was settled by Spaniards in 1716. Many of the adobe cottages have seen better days, but there are shops, modest galleries, taco stands, two fine restaurants (☞ Dining, *below*), and the famous San Francisco de Asís Church. ⊠ *Paseo del Pueblo Norte (NM 68), about 4 mi south of Taos Plaza.*

OFF THE BEATEN PATH

GHOST RANCH – Georgia O'Keeffe wrote, "When I first saw the Abiquiú house it was a ruin. . . . As I climbed and walked about in the ruin I found a patio with a very pretty well house and a bucket to draw up water. It was a good-sized patio with a long wall with a door on one side. That wall with a door in it was something I had to have. It took me 10 years to get it—three more years to fix the house up so I could live in it—and after that the wall with the door was painted many times." The artist first stayed on the hauntingly beautiful Ghost Ranch, owned by a family who let her use it to paint. In 1949 she moved to her permanent ranch in Abiquiú, 20 mi south of Ghost Ranch, and continued to paint her dreamy landscapes and beguiling still lifes. O'Keeffe, who died in 1986 at the age of 98, left special provisions in her will to ensure that the houses would never be public monuments or tourist arenas. The rocky desert vistas between Ghost Ranch and Abiquiú are all that remain accessible to the public; her Abiquiú home is rarely open. The **Ghost Ranch Living Museum** occupies a portion of Ghost Ranch, but rather than commemorate O'Keeffe, its exhibits are nature-oriented. Almost every type of animal that calls northern New Mexico home lives at this site, including eagles and mountain lions. The museum is also a botanical garden and serves as the Carson National Forest's environmental education center. ⊠ *60 mi southwest of Taos; take NM 68 south to Española and pick up U.S. 84 west to Abiquiú; look for a dirt road off U.S. 84 marked with a cattle-skull highway sign. Museum: off U.S. 84, Abiquiú,* ☎ *505/685–4312.* ☜ *Donation $3.* ☉ *Tues.–Sun. 8–4:30.*

⑫ **San Francisco de Asís Church.** The Spanish Mission–style church was erected in the 18th century as a spiritual and physical refuge from raiding Apaches, Utes, and Comanches. By the 1970s it had deteriorated, but it was rebuilt in 1979 by community volunteers using traditional adobe bricks. The earthy, clean lines of the exterior walls and supporting bulwarks have inspired generations of painters and photographers. The late-afternoon light provides the best exposure of the heavily buttressed rear of the church; morning light is best for the front. Bells in the twin belfries call Taoseños to services on Sunday and holidays. In the parish hall nearby, a 15-minute video presentation every half hour describes the history and restoration of the church and explains the mysterious painting, *Shadow of the Cross*, on which each evening the shadow of a cross appears over Christ's shoulder. Scientific studies made on the canvas and the paint pigments cannot explain the phenomenon. ⊠ *NM 68, 500 yards south of NM 518, Ranchos de Taos,* ☎ *505/758–2754.* ☜ *$1.* ☉ *Mon.–Sat. 9–4; Sun. and holy days during morning church services: Mass at 7 (in Spanish), 9, and 11:30.*

Taos Pueblo and Rio Grande Gorge

Numbers in the text correspond to numbers in the margin and on the Taos Pueblo and the Enchanted Circle map.

A Good Drive

Drive 3 mi north on Paseo del Pueblo Norte (NM 68), and keep your eyes peeled for the signs on the right, beyond the post office, directing you to **Taos Pueblo** ⑬. After exploring the pueblo, continue your drive by returning south on NM 68 to U.S. 64 west. Drive to the traffic light and continue to follow U.S. 64 west to the **Rio Grande Gorge Bridge** ⑭, a stunning marriage of natural wonder and human engineering. Take along sturdy hiking shoes and plenty of water and snacks for an invigorating walk down into the gorge. But remember that what goes down must come up, and it's an arduous path.

TIMING

Plan on spending two hours at the pueblo. Taos can get hot in summer, but if you visit the pueblo in the morning, you'll avoid the heat and the crowds. Winters can be cold and windy, so dress warmly. The best time to visit in any season is during one of the ceremonial dances. But set aside several hours, because the ceremonies, though they are worth the wait, never start on time. A half hour should be enough time to take in the grandeur of the Rio Grande Gorge Bridge.

Sights to See

🖐 ⑭ **Rio Grande Gorge Bridge.** It's a breathtaking experience to see the gorge with the Rio Grande flowing 650 ft below. The bridge is the second-highest expansion bridge in the country. Hold on to your camera and eyeglasses when looking down, and watch out for low-flying planes. The Taos Municipal Airport is close by, and daredevil private pilots have been known to challenge one another to fly under the bridge.

★ 🖐 ⑬ **Taos Pueblo.** For nearly 1,000 years the mud-and-straw adobe walls—several feet thick in places—of Taos Pueblo have sheltered the customs and way of life of the Taos-Tiwa Native Americans. A United Nations World Heritage Site, this is the largest multistory pueblo structure in the United States. The two main buildings, Hlauuma (north house) and Hlaukwima (south house), separated by a creek, are believed to be of a similar age, probably constructed between 1000 and 1450. The dwellings have common walls but no con-

Taos Pueblo and the Enchanted Circle

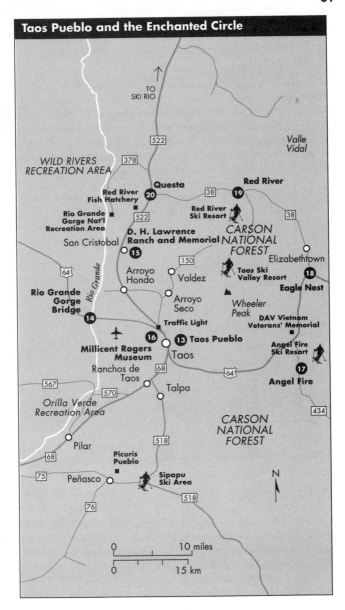

TO
SKI RIO

*Valle
Vidal*

522

378

*WILD RIVERS
RECREATION AREA*

Red River
Red River
Fish Hatchery
Questa **20**
38 **19**

**Rio Grande
Gorge Nat'l
Recreation Area**
522
Red River
Ski Resort
38

**D. H. Lawrence
Ranch and Memorial**
San Cristobal **15**
*CARSON
NATIONAL
FOREST*

150
Taos Ski
Valley Resort
Elizabethtown

64
Arroyo
Hondo
Valdez
18
Eagle Nest

Rio Grande
Arroyo
Seco
*Wheeler
Peak*

**Rio Grande
Gorge
Bridge**
14
Traffic Light **16** **13** **Taos Pueblo**
DAV Vietnam
Veterans' Memorial

**Millicent Rogers
Museum**
Taos
Angel Fire
Ski Resort
17

Ranchos de
Taos
68
64
Angel Fire

567
570
Talpa
434

*Orilla Verde
Recreation Area*
518
*CARSON
NATIONAL
FOREST*

68
Pilar
**Picuris
Pueblo**
**Sipapu
Ski Area**
N

75
Peñasco
518

76

0 | 10 miles
0 | 15 km

necting doorways—the Tiwas gained access only from the top, via ladders that were retrieved after entering. Small buildings and corrals are scattered about.

The pueblo today appears much as it did when the first Spanish explorers arrived in New Mexico in 1540. The adobe walls glistening with mica caused the conquistadors to believe they had discovered one of the fabled Seven Cities of Gold. The outside surfaces are continuously maintained by replastering with thin layers of mud, and the interior walls are frequently coated with thin washes of white earth to keep them clean and bright. The roofs of each of the five-story structures are supported by large timbers, or vigas, hauled down from the mountain forests. Rotted vigas are replaced as needed. Pine or aspen *latillas* (smaller pieces of wood) are placed side by side between the vigas; the entire roof is then packed with dirt.

Even after 400 years of Spanish and Anglo presence in Taos, inside the pueblo the traditional Native American way of life has endured. Tribal custom allows no electricity or running water in Hlauuma and Hlaukwima, where varying numbers (usually fewer than 100) of Taos Native Americans live full time. About 2,000 others live in conventional homes on the pueblo's 95,000 acres. The crystal-clear waters of the Rio Pueblo de Taos, originating high above in the mountains at the sacred Blue Lake, are the primary source of water for drinking and irrigation. Bread is still baked in *hornos* (outdoor domed ovens). Artisans of the Taos Pueblo produce and sell (tax free) traditionally handcrafted wares such as mica-flecked pottery and silver jewelry. Great hunters, the Taos Native Americans are also known for their work with animal skins, and their excellent moccasins, boots, and drums.

Although the population is about 90% Catholic, the Tiwa, like most of the Pueblo people, also maintain their native religious traditions. At Christmas and other sacred holidays, for instance, immediately after Mass, Native American dancers, dressed in seasonal sacred garb, proceed down the church aisle, drums beating and rattles shaking, to begin their own religious rites.

The pueblo Church of San Geronimo, or St. Jerome, the patron saint of Taos Pueblo, was completed in 1850 to replace the original, which was destroyed by the U.S. Army in 1847 during the Mexican War. With its flowing lines, arched portal, and twin bell towers, the church is a popular subject of photographers and artists (though the taking of photographs inside is discouraged).

The public is invited to certain ceremonial dances held throughout the year: January 1, Turtle Dance; January 6, Buffalo or Deer Dance; May 3, Feast of Santa Cruz Foot Race and Corn Dance; June 13, Feast of San Antonio Corn Dance; June 24, Feast of San Juan Corn Dance; July 2 weekend, Taos Pueblo Powwow; July 25–26, Feast of Santa Ana and Santiago Corn Dance; September 29–30, Feast of San Geronimo Sunset Dance; Christmas Eve, the Procession; Christmas Day, Deer Dance. While you're at the pueblo certain rules must be observed: Respect the RESTRICTED AREA signs that protect the privacy of residents and sites of native religious practices; do not enter private homes or open any doors not clearly labeled as curio shops; do not photograph tribal members without asking permission; do not enter the cemetery grounds; and do not wade in the Rio Pueblo de Taos, which is considered sacred and is the community's sole source of drinking water. ⊠ *Head to the right off Paseo del Pueblo Norte just past the Best Western Kachina Lodge,* ☏ *505/758–9593.* 🎟 *Tourist fees: $8 per vehicle (for parking), plus $4 per person, $30 for tour buses (plus $4 per passenger); still-camera permit $10, video-camera permit $10; $75 to sketch; $150 to paint.* ☉ *Apr.–Nov., daily 8–4; Oct.–Mar., daily 8:30–4. Closed for funerals, religious ceremonies, and for two-month "quiet time" in late winter or early spring; call ahead before planning to visit at this time.*

NEED A BREAK?	Look for signs that read FRY BREAD on dwellings in the pueblo: You can enter the kitchen and buy a piece of fresh fry bread—bread dough that is flattened and deep-fried until puffy and golden brown and then topped with honey or powdered sugar.

The Enchanted Circle

Some clever marketers conceived the moniker the Enchanted Circle to describe the territory accessed by the roads (U.S. 64 to NM 522 to NM 38 back to U.S. 64) that form an 84-mi loop north from Taos and back to town, but it's likely you won't argue with their choice. A day trip through the Enchanted Circle includes a glorious panorama of alpine valleys and the towering mountains of the lush Carson National Forest. You can see all the major sights listed below on one drive, but two itineraries are recommended, the first one short and oriented toward Taos's artistic and literary past, the second longer and focused on the natural setting.

Numbers in the text correspond to numbers in the margin and on the Taos Pueblo and the Enchanted Circle map.

A Good Drive

Take U.S. 64 northwest out of Taos; at the traffic light head north on NM 522. Keep an eye out for the clearly marked sign that points to the **D. H. Lawrence Ranch and Memorial** ⑮. The memorial may be visited, but the other buildings on the ranch are closed to the public. Head back south to Taos along NM 522 about 5 or 6 mi to the traffic light. At that corner watch for the signs directing you to the **Millicent Rogers Museum** ⑯. Keep a sharp watch for signs and turnoff. This rural road eventually connects back onto Upper Ranchitos Road. (If you miss the turn, go back into town, pick up NM 240 [Ranchitos Road], and turn left onto Upper Ranchitos. You'll feel as if you're driving off the edge of the earth, but after about 4 mi or so you'll see the big adobe wall and the sign for the museum.)

TIMING

The D. H. Lawrence Memorial takes about a half hour to visit. An hour or two at the Millicent Rogers Museum should be enough time to take in its galleries and exhibits.

A Good Drive

Traveling east from Taos along U.S. 64, you'll soon be winding through Taos Canyon, climbing your way toward 9,000-ft-high Palo Flechado Pass. On the other side of the pass, after about 25 mi you will come to **Angel Fire** ⑰, a ski resort. Continue east on U.S. 64 about 14 mi to tiny **Eagle Nest** ⑱, an old-fashioned ski-resort village. Next take NM 38 going northwest and head over Bobcat Pass, a tad under 10,000 ft in elevation, about 16 mi to **Red River** ⑲. From Red River the Enchanted Circle heads west about 12 mi to scenic **Questa** ⑳. The **Red River Hatchery** is about 5 mi south of Questa on NM 522. From the hatchery, it's about 15 mi to Taos, south on NM 522.

If you have the time, about 8 mi south of the hatchery you can take the dirt road off NM 522 that leads to the **D. H. Lawrence Ranch and Memorial** ⑮. Continue south on NM 522 at the traffic light to get to the **Millicent Rogers Museum** ⑯.

TIMING

Leave early in the morning and plan to spend the entire day on this trip, spending as much time as you wish in each town. During ski season you may want to make it an overnight trip and get in a day of skiing (☞ Skiing *in* Outdoor Activities and Sports, *below*). In spring, summer, and fall your drive should be free of snow and ice. A sunny winter day will yield some lovely scenery (but if there's snow on the ground, don't forget your sunglasses).

Sights To See

❶⑰ **Angel Fire.** For hundreds of years a long, empty valley and the fall meeting grounds of the Ute Native Americans, the Angel Fire area is a busy ski resort these days. A prominent landmark is the **DAV Vietnam Veterans Memorial**, a 50-ft-high gull wing–shape monument built in 1971 by D. Victor Westphall, whose son David was killed in Vietnam. The memorial's textured surface, which captures the dazzling, colorful reflections of the New Mexican mountains, changes constantly with the sun's movement. ⊠ *U.S. 64, 25 mi east of Taos.*

Carson National Forest. The national forest that surrounds Taos spans almost 200 mi across northern New Mexico and encompasses mountains, lakes, streams, villages, and much of the Enchanted Circle. Hiking, skiing, horseback riding, mountain biking, backpacking, trout fishing, boating, and wildflower viewing are among the popular activities here. The forest is home to big-game animals and many species of smaller animals and songbirds; you can see them at the **Ghost Ranch Living Museum** (☞ Ghost Ranch, *above*). **Wheeler Peak** (☞ *below*) is a designated wilderness area where travel is restricted to foot or horseback. Contact the Carson National Forest for maps, safety guidelines, and conditions. ⊠ *Forest Service Building, 208 Cruz Alta Rd., Taos 87571,* ☎ *505/758–6200.* ☉ *Weekdays 8–4:30.*

⑮ D. H. Lawrence Ranch and Memorial. The English writer David Herbert Lawrence lived in Taos for about 22 months during a three-year period between 1922 and 1925. He and his wife, Frieda, arrived in Taos at the behest of Mabel Dodge Luhan, who collected famous writers and artists the way some people collect butterflies. Luhan provided them a place to live, Kiowa Ranch, on 160 acres in the mountains north of Taos. Rustic and remote, it's known as the D. H. Lawrence Ranch, though Lawrence never actually owned it. Nearby is the smaller cabin where Dorothy Brett, the traveling companion of the Lawrences, stayed. The houses, owned by the University of New Mexico, are not open to the public, but you can visit the nearby D. H. Lawrence Memorial (formerly Shrine, but apparently that name rattled local religious types) on wooded Lobo Mountain. A white shedlike structure, it is simple and unimposing. The writer fell ill while visiting France and died in a sanatorium there in 1930. Five years later Frieda had Lawrence's body disinterred, cremated, and brought back to Taos. Frieda Lawrence is buried, as was her wish, in front of the memorial. ⊠ *NM 522 (follow signed dirt road from the highway), San Cristobal,* ☎ *505/776–2245.* ☞ *Free.* ☉ *Daily.*

⑱ Eagle Nest. Thousands of acres of national forest surround this funky village, population 189, elevation 8,090 ft. The shops and other buildings here evoke New Mexico's mining heritage. Four miles north of Eagle's Nest on NM 38 is **Elizabethtown,** a former gold mining village with sweeping landscapes, a few ruins, and a very shady past—in the 19th century some people died here under mysterious circumstances. ⊠ *NM 38, 14 mi north of Angel Fire.*

⑯ Millicent Rogers Museum. More than 5,000 pieces of Native American and Hispanic art, the core of Standard Oil heiress Millicent Rogers's private collection, are on exhibit here: baskets, blankets, rugs, jewelry, kachina dolls, carvings, paintings, and rare religious and secular artifacts. A recent acquisition of major importance is the pottery and ceramics of Maria Martinez and other potters from San Ildefonso Pueblo (☞ Chapter 2). Docents conduct tours on request, and the museum hosts lectures, films, workshops, and demonstrations. ⊠ *NM 522, south of U.S. 64 (from Taos Plaza head north on Paseo del Pueblo Norte and left at blinking traffic light),* ☎ *505/758–2462.* ☞ *$6.* ☉ *Mon.–Sat. 10–5, Sun. noon–5; closed Mon. Nov.–Mar.*

❷⓿ **Questa.** Literally "hill" in the "Heart of the Sangre de Cristo Mountains," Questa is a quiet village nestled between the Red River and Taos amid some of the most striking mountain country in New Mexico. **St. Anthony's Church,** built of adobe with 5-ft-thick walls and viga ceilings, is about 12 mi from Red River. Questa's **Cabresto Lake,** in the Carson National Forest about 23 mi north of Taos, has trout fishing and boating and is open from about June to October. You'll need a four-wheel-drive vehicle to access the lake because there are 2 mi of narrow, deeply rutted roads along the way.

❶⓽ **Red River.** A major ski resort, Red River, elevation 8,750 ft, came into being as a miners' boom town during the 19th century, taking its name from the river whose mineral content gave it a rich, rosy color. When the gold petered out, Red River died, only to be rediscovered in the 1920s by migrants who were escaping the dust storms in the Great Plains states. An Old West flavor remains: Main Street shoot-outs, an authentic melodrama, and square dancing and two-stepping are among the diversions here. Because of its many country dances and festivals, Red River is affectionately called "The New Mexico Home of the Texas Two-Step." The bustling little downtown area contains shops and sportswear boutiques. ⊠ *Off NM 38,* ☎ *505/ 776–5510 for resort reservations.*

☾ **Red River Hatchery.** At this engaging facility you can feed freshwater trout and learn how they're hatched, reared, stocked, and controlled. The visitor center has displays and exhibits, a show pond, and a machine that dispenses fish food. The self-guided tour can last anywhere from 20 to 90 minutes, depending on how enraptured you become. There's a picnic area on the grounds. ⊠ *NM 522, 5 mi south of Questa,* ☎ *505/586–0222.* ☞ *Free.* ☺ *Daily 8–5.*

OFF THE
BEATEN
PATH

WHEELER PEAK – Part of the Sangre de Cristo Mountains, 13,000-ft-high Wheeler is the tallest spot in New Mexico. The 7-mi trail to the peak begins at the Taos Ski Valley, 15 mi northeast of Taos on County Road 150. Only experienced hikers should tackle this strenuous trail. Dress warmly even in summer, take plenty of water and food, and pay attention to *all* warnings and instructions distributed by the forest rangers.

DINING

For a place as isolated as Taos, the dining scene is surprisingly varied. You can find the usual coffee shops and Mexican-style eateries, but also restaurants serving creatively prepared Continental, Italian, and Southwestern cuisine. At two of the area's most casual places, Cafe Fresen in Arroyo Seco and Bravo!, which is 2 mi south of Taos Plaza, you can grab a sophisticated bite to eat in or to go.

CATEGORY	COST*
$$$$	over $30
$$$	$20–$30
$$	$10–$20
$	under $10

per person, excluding drinks, service, and sales tax (6.75%).

Taos

American

$$–$$$ ✗ **Ogelvie's Bar and Grille.** On the second floor of an old two-story adobe building on the east side of the Taos Plaza, Ogelvie's is the perfect spot for people-watching from on high, especially from the outdoor patio in summer. You won't find any culinary surprises here, just dependable meat-and-potato dishes. The sure bets are Angus beef, grilled Rocky Mountain trout, and meat or cheese enchiladas. ⊠ *East side of Taos Plaza,* ☎ *505/758–8866. Reservations not accepted. AE, DC, MC, V.*

89

Apple Tree, **5**
Bent Street Deli, **6**
Bravo!, **13**
Casa Cordova, **3**
Casa de
Valdez, **14**
Casa Fresen
Bakery, **4**
Doc Martin's, **7**
Fred's Place, **11**
Jacquelina's, **15**
Joseph's
Table, **17**
La Folie, **8**
Lambert's of
Taos, **12**
Ogelvie's Bar and
Grille, **9**
Roberto's, **10**
Stakeout Grill
and Bar, **18**
Tim's Chile
Connection, **2**
Trading Post
Cafe, **16**
Villa Fontana, **1**

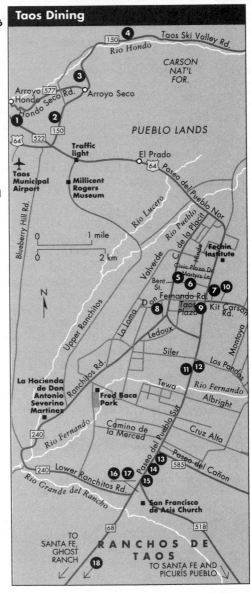

Taos Dining

Contemporary

$$$–
$$$$ ✕ **Doc Martin's.** The restaurant of the Taos Inn takes its
name from the building's original owner, a local physician
who performed operations and delivered babies in rooms
that now are the dining areas. Among the signature creations
are the piñon-crusted salmon, the lacquered duck, and the
Aztec chocolate mousse with roasted-banana sauce. The wine
list has won awards from *Wine Spectator* and other orga-
nizations. ⊠ *Taos Inn, 125 Paseo del Pueblo Norte,* ☎ *505/
758–1977. MC, V.*

$$$ ✕ **Apple Tree.** Named for the large tree in the courtyard,
this is a great lunch and early dinner spot in a historic adobe
a block from the Plaza. The food is a bit overpriced but
fresh—among the well-crafted dishes are grilled lamb and
chicken fajitas. Sunday brunch is served from 10 to 3. ⊠
123 Bent St., ☎ *505/758–1900. AE, D, DC, MC, V.*

$$$ ✕ **La Folie.** The French-influenced menu changes often at
this restaurant with a welcoming courtyard. Appetizers
might include an Asian-spiced soft-shell crab with chile aioli
or a baked goat-cheese salad. Among the entrées might be
smoked chicken and cherry sausage with saffron fettuccine
or seared duck breast with fresh herb risotto and aspara-
gus. Adjacent to the main dining room is a tapas bar. Up-
stairs are guest quarters ($$). Upon request the chef will
bring dinner to your room for the ultimate in intimate din-
ing. ⊠ *122 Dona Luz, between Don Fernando Rd. and Ranchitos Rd.,* ☎ *505/751–1738. AE, MC, V. Closed Mon.*

$$–$$$ ✕ **Lambert's of Taos.** The signature dishes at this restau-
rant 2½ blocks south of the Plaza include crab cakes and
pepper-crusted lamb. California's finest vintages receive
top billing on the wine list. The desserts are tasty. ⊠ *Randall House, 309 Paseo del Pueblo Sur,* ☎ *505/758–1009.
AE, DC, MC, V. No lunch weekends.*

$–$$ ✕ **Bravo!** Short on atmosphere but by no means tacky, this
restaurant and full bar inside an upscale grocery store and
beer and wine shop is a great stop for gourmet picnic fix-
ings or an on-site meal. The fare is nothing if not varied—
you can feast on anything from a turkey sandwich to
escargots—and there's a children's menu to boot. The beer
and wine selection is formidable. ⊠ *1353A Paseo del
Pueblo Sur,* ☎ *505/758–8100. Reservations not accepted.
MC, V. Closed Sun.*

Deli

$$–$$$ ✕ **Bent Street Deli.** Great soups, sandwiches, salads, and desserts (cheesecake and other sweet treats) are the trademarks of the small and unassuming Bent Street Deli, which serves beer, wine, and gourmet coffees. Reubens are on the menu for East Coasters and others who can't live without a dose of pastrami. Dinners are a little fancier: fresh salmon, Sumatra primavera pasta with Indonesian peanut sauce, or shrimp in pesto sauce. Breakfast is served until 11. ⊠ *120 Bent St.,* ☎ *505/758–5787. MC, V. Closed Sun.*

Southwestern

$$–$$$ ✕ **Casa de Valdez.** A large A-frame building with wood-panel walls and beamed ceilings, Casa de Valdez has the feel of a mountain lodge. The tables and chairs are handmade, as are the colorful drapes on the windows. Owner-chef Peter Valdez specializes in hickory-smoked barbecues, charcoal-grilled steaks, and regional New Mexican cuisine. ⊠ *1401 Paseo del Pueblo Sur,* ☎ *505/758–8777. AE, D, MC, V. Closed Wed.*

$$–$$$ ✕ **Jacquelina's.** Chef Chuck La Mendole creates delicate
★ food and presents it superbly. The grilled salmon with tomatillo salsa is top-notch, as is the barbecued shrimp with *poblano* (a dark green, rich-tasting chile, ranging from mild to fiery) corn salsa. It's the place to go for great upscale Southwestern food, knowledgeable service, and comfortable surroundings. ⊠ *1541 Paseo del Pueblo Sur,* ☎ *505/751–0399. MC, V. Closed Mon. No lunch Sat.*

$$ ✕ **Fred's Place.** Eccentric decorations—carved crucifixes and santos and a ceiling mural of hell—set a quirky tone at this hip spot with a congenial staff. You may have to stand in line at popular Fred's, but you'll find you haven't waited in vain when you taste the subtly prepared northern New Mexican specialties like *carne adovada* (meat, marinated in a spicy sauce) and blue-corn enchiladas. ⊠ *332 Paseo del Pueblo Sur,* ☎ *505/758–0514. Reservations not accepted. MC, V. Closed Sun. No lunch.*

$ ✕ **Roberto's.** Bobby and Patsy Garcia serve creative native New Mexican dishes from recipes handed down through the Garcia family for generations. The chiles rellenos are particularly good. Art and cherished family antiques fill the three intimate Southwestern-style dining rooms. ⊠ *122B*

E. Kit Carson Rd., ☎ 505/758–2434. AE, D, MC, V.
Closed Tues.

Ranchos de Taos and Points South

American

$$$–
$$$$
✕ **Stakeout Grill and Bar.** On Outlaw Hill in the foothills
of the Sangre de Cristo Mountains, this old adobe home-
stead has 100-mi-long views and sunsets that dazzle. The
sturdy fare includes New York strip steaks, filet mignon, roast
prime rib, shrimp scampi, swordfish steaks, duck, chicken,
and daily pasta specials. The restaurant's decor will take you
back to the days of the Wild West. ⊠ *Stakeout Dr., east of
NM 68 (look for the huge cowboy hat), 8½ mi south of Taos
Plaza,* ☎ *505/758–2042. AE, D, DC, MC, V.*

Contemporary

$$$–
$$$$
✕ **Joseph's Table.** The spiffily funky, moodily lighted dining rooms at Joseph's set the stage for unfussy Italian-ori-
ented fare like gnocchi stuffed with white-truffle paste,
roasted duck, and pepper steak with garlic mashed red
potatoes. The first-rate desserts are more ornate. ⊠ *4167
Paseo del Pueblo Sur (NM 68), Ranchos de Taos,* ☎ *505/
751–4512. AE, D, DC, MC, V. Closed Mon. No lunch.*

$$$–
$$$$
★
✕ **Trading Post Cafe.** A postmodern Western ambience,
impeccable service, and an imaginative menu have made
the Trading Post the most popular dining spot in Ranchos
de Taos. The perfectly marinated salmon gravlax appetizer
is exceptional and the paella is a bounty for two. The
desserts—try the homemade raspberry sorbet or the flan—
are delicious. ⊠ *4179 Paseo del Pueblo Sur (NM 68), Ran-
chos de Taos,* ☎ *505/758–5089. MC, V. Closed Sun.*

The Enchanted Circle

American

$$$–
$$$$
✕ **Casa Cordova.** The cozy Cordova, an L-shape adobe
building with a wooden portal, serves classic food in a
large dining area that has two fireplaces. Menu highlights
include seafood, steaks, and Mexican specialties. ⊠ *Taos
Ski Valley Rd. (County Rd. 150) at Arroyo Seco,* ☎ *505/
776–2500. AE, D, MC, V. Closed Sun.*

Contemporary

$$–$$$ ✕ **Tim's Chile Connection.** Young skiers flock to this place for beer, country-western music, and Tim's stick-to-your-ribs Southwestern blue-corn tortillas, homemade salsa, buffalo burgers and steaks, and fajitas. The tab is pricey for what you get, but the margaritas are monumental and delicious—even memorable. ⊠ *Taos Ski Valley Rd. (County Rd. 150),* ☏ *505/776–8787. AE, MC, V.*

Deli

$$ ✕ **Casa Fresen Bakery.** Locals love this bakery, espresso bar,
★ and Italian deli tucked away in Arroyo Seco. You can sample imported cheeses the likes of which are usually found only in New York City, along with fresh pâtés and specialty meats. From the ovens come breads, muffins, croissants, and pastries. The sandwiches are works of art—the take-out lunches and picnic baskets are perfect for long days in the countryside. ⊠ *Taos Ski Valley Rd. (County Rd. 150),* ☏ *505/776–2969. MC, V.*

Italian

$$$$ ✕ **Villa Fontana.** Entering this restaurant that serves north-
★ ern Italian cuisine is like walking into a sophisticated Italian country inn: warm coral walls, candlelit dining, gleaming hardwood tables, and starched linens. Notable dishes include grilled whole sole and seasonal game like venison and pheasant. The staff members are so well trained they seem like ballet dancers going through their paces. Lunch is served in the garden. ⊠ *NM 522, 5 mi north of Taos Plaza,* ☏ *505/758–5800. AE, D, DC, MC, V. Closed Sun. No lunch Nov.–May.*

LODGING

The hotels and motels along NM 68 (Paseo del Pueblo Sur and Norte) suit every need and budget; rates vary little between big-name chains and smaller establishments. Expect higher rates during the ski season (usually from late December to early April) and in July and August. Reservations are recommended during these times. Skiers have many deluxe resorts to choose from, in town and on the slopes.

The best deals in town are the bed-and-breakfasts. Mostly family-owned, they provide personal service, delicious breakfasts, and many extras that hotels charge for. The B&Bs are often in old adobes that have been refurbished with style and flair.

CATEGORY	COST*
$$$$	over $150
$$$	$100–$150
$$	$65–$100
$	under $65

All prices are for a standard double room, excluding 3.5% city room tax or 3% county room tax, 6.9% city sales tax or 6.3% county sales tax, and service charges.

Downtown Taos

$$$–
$$$$ 🏨 **Fechin Inn.** This graceful Pueblo Revival structure on the grounds of the Fechin Institute (to which guests have free admission) is adjacent to Kit Carson Memorial Park. Painter Nicolai Fechin's daughter, Eya, participated in the planning; Fechin reproductions adorn the rooms and hallways, and the woodwork in the large, comfortable lobby is based on the artist's designs. A generous breakfast is available every morning in the lobby, as are cocktails in evening. Rooms are comfortable, if nondescript; most have private balconies or patios. Pets are welcome. ⊠ *227 Paseo del Pueblo Norte, 87571,* ☎ *505/751–1000 or 800/811–2933,* 𝔽𝔸𝕏 *505/751–7338. 85 rooms and suites. Massage, exercise room, ski storage, meeting rooms, free parking. Continental breakfast. AE, D, DC, MC, V.*

$$$–
$$$$ 🏨 **Hacienda Inn on La Loma Plaza.** The walls surrounding this Spanish-style inn (formerly the Taos Hacienda Inn) built in the early 1800s were designed to protect a small enclave of settlers from invasions. The rambling structure, listed on the National Register of Historic Places, has rooms with Southwestern accents; the sitting areas all have fireplaces. The comfortable living room contains a well-stocked library and an interesting collection of antique cameras. ⊠ *315 Ranchitos Rd. (Box 4159), 87571,* ☎ *505/758–1717 or 800/530–3040,* 𝔽𝔸𝕏 *505/751–0155. 5 rooms, 2 artist studios with kitchenettes. Full breakfast. AE, MC, V.*

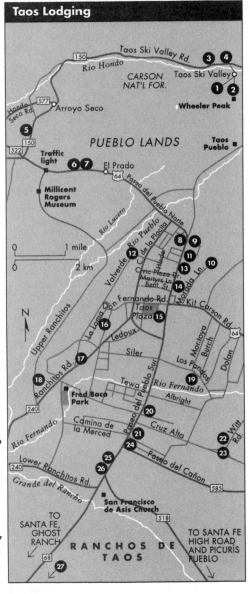

$$–$$$$ 🏨 **Mabel Dodge Luhan House.** This National Historic Landmark was once the home of the heiress who became a professional friend to the literati of the area. Guests from pre-B&B days included D. H. and Frieda Lawrence, Georgia O'Keeffe, and Willa Cather. The main house contains nine guest rooms, and there are eight more in a separate guest house, as well as a two-bedroom cottage. The inn is frequently used for literary, artistic, cultural, and educational meetings and workshops. Don't expect glamour—this is one of the most basic B&Bs in town. The buildings are rumpled and frayed and the stairs creak. ⊠ *Box 3400, 240 Morada La., 87571, ☎ 505/758–9456 or 800/846–2235, FAX 505/751–0431. 12 rooms with bath, 5 without bath, 1 cottage. Meeting rooms. Full breakfast. AE, MC, V.*

$$$ 🏨 **Best Western Kachina Lodge de Taos.** Down the road from Taos Pueblo and minutes from the Taos Plaza, this hotel is in a two-story Pueblo-style adobe. Nightly from Memorial Day to Labor Day a troupe from Taos Pueblo performs ritual dances outside by firelight. The kachina theme is carried throughout, and guest rooms continue the Native American motif with handmade and hand-painted furnishings and colorful bedspreads. ⊠ *413 Paseo del Pueblo Norte (Box NN), 87571, ☎ 505/758–2275 or 800/522–4462, FAX 505/758–9207. 118 rooms. Restaurant, bar, coffee shop, pool, hot tub, shops. AE, D, DC, MC, V.*

$$$ 🏨 **Casa de las Chimeneas.** Regional art, tile hearths, French
★   doors, and traditional viga ceilings are among the design elements of note at the "House of Chimneys," 2½ blocks from the Plaza and secluded behind thick adobe walls. Each room in the 1912 structure has a private entrance, a fireplace, handmade New Mexican furniture, and a tile bar stocked with complimentary juices, sodas, and mineral waters. All rooms overlook the formal gardens and fountains. The two-course breakfasts might include an artichoke-mushroom omelette with corn muffins. ⊠ *405 Cordoba Rd. (Box 5303), 87571, ☎ 505/758–4777, FAX 505/758–3976. 5 rooms, 1 suite. Minibars, outdoor hot tub, in-room VCRs, sauna, exercise room, laundry service. Full breakfast. No smoking. AE, MC, V.*

$$$–   🏨 **Casa Europa.** Its original adobe bricks and wood viga ceil-
$$$$ ing enhance the pastoral mood of this classic estate on 6 acres with views of pastures and mountains. European antiques

and Southwestern pieces decorate the rooms. The main guest areas are light and airy with comfortable chairs to relax in and listen to the fire crackle. Breakfasts are elaborate, and complimentary homemade afternoon pastries are served daily except during the ski season, when they're replaced by evening hors d'oeuvres. ⊠ *840 Upper Ranchitos Rd., HC 68 (Box 3F), 87571,* ☎ *505/758–9798 or 888/758–9798. 6 double rooms. Hot tub, sauna. Full breakfast. MC, V.*

$$$ 🖬 **Comfort Suites.** Each unit at this complex next door to the Sagebrush Inn contains a living room with a sofa bed, a bedroom with a king- and a queen-size bed, a television in both rooms, a microwave oven, a coffeemaker, and a refrigerator. ⊠ *1500 Paseo del Pueblo Sur (Box 1268), 87571,* ☎ *505/751–1555 or 888/751–1555. 60 suites. Hot tub, pool. Continental breakfast. AE, D, DC, MC, V.*

$$$ 🖬 **Holiday Inn Don Fernando de Taos.** The accommodations at this hotel with a Pueblo-style design are grouped around central courtyards and connected by walkways. Appointed with hand-carved New Mexican furnishings, the rooms have kiva-style fireplaces. ⊠ *1005 Paseo del Pueblo Sur, 87571,* ☎ *505/758–4444 or 800/759–2736,* 🖷 *505/758–0055. 124 rooms. Restaurant, bar, lounge, pool, hot tub, tennis court. AE, D, DC, MC, V.*

$$$ 🖬 **Rancho Ramada Inn de Taos.** More Taos than Ramada, the two-story adobe-style hotel welcomes you with a lobby fireplace, desert colors, Western art, and Native American pottery. The rooms have an inviting Southwestern-style flavor. ⊠ *615 Paseo del Pueblo Sur, 87571,* ☎ *505/758–2900 or 800/659–8267,* 🖷 *505/758–1662. 124 rooms. Dining room, lounge, pool, meeting rooms. AE, D, DC, MC, V.*

$$$ 🖬 **San Geronimo Lodge.** On a small street off Kit Carson Road, this lodge built in 1925 sits on 2½ acres that front the majestic Taos Mountain and back up to the Carson National Forest. A balcony library, attractive grounds, many rooms with fireplaces, and two rooms designed for people with disabilities are among the draws. The hotel staff will arrange ski packages. ⊠ *1101 Witt Rd., 87571,* ☎ *505/751–3776 or 800/894–4119,* 🖷 *505/751–1493. 18 rooms. Pool, hot tub, massage. AE, D, DC, MC, V.*

$$$ 🖬 **Taos Inn.** Mere steps from Taos Plaza, this hotel is listed in the National Register of Historic Places. The guest rooms are pleasant and comfortable, and in summer there's dining alfresco on the patio. The lobby, which also serves as seating for the Adobe Bar, is built around an old town well, from which a fountain bubbles forth. Many shops and restaurants are within walking distance of the inn. ⊠ *125 Paseo del Pueblo Norte, 87571,* ☎ *505/758–2233 or 800/ 826–7466,* ℻ *505/758–5776. 36 rooms. Restaurant, bar, lounge, library. AE, DC, MC, V.*

$$–$$$ 🏨 **Brooks Street Inn.** An elaborately carved corbel arch, the handiwork of Japanese carpenter Yaichikido, spans the entrance to a shaded, walled garden. Fluffy pillows, fresh flowers, and paintings by local artists are among the graceful notes in the rooms. Blue-corn pancakes with pineapple salsa, stuffed French toast with an apricot glaze, and other home-baked delights are served at breakfast, along with coffee or espresso drinks. In warm weather breakfast is served at umbrella-shaded tables on the patio; in winter it's served by the fireplace. ⊠ *119 Brooks St. (Box 4954), 87571,* ☎ *505/758–1489 or 800/758–1489. 6 rooms. Full breakfast. No smoking. AE, MC, V.*

$$–$$$ 🏨 **La Posada de Taos.** A couple of blocks from Taos Plaza, this provincial adobe has beam ceilings, a portal, kiva-style fireplaces, and the intimacy of a private hacienda. Five of the guest rooms are in the main house; the sixth is a separate cottage with a queen-size four-poster bed, a sitting room, and a fireplace—a setting cozy and pretty enough to earn the name *La Casa de la Luna de Miel* (The Honeymoon House). The rooms have mountain views or face a flowering courtyard; all but one of the rooms have adobe fireplaces. Innkeepers Bill Swan and Nancy Brooks-Swan prepare hearty breakfasts. ⊠ *309 Juanita La. (Box 1118), 87571,* ☎ *505/758–8164 or 800/645–4803,* ℻ *505/751– 3294. 5 rooms, 1 cottage. Full breakfast. No credit cards.*

$$–$$$ 🏨 **Old Taos Guesthouse.** Once a ramshackle adobe hacienda, this homey B&B has been completely and lovingly outfitted with the owners' hand-carved doors and furniture, Western artifacts, and antiques. Some rooms have the smallest bathrooms you'll ever encounter, but have private entrances and some have fireplaces. There are 80-mi views from the outdoor hot tub. The owners welcome families. ⊠ *1028 Witt Rd. (Box 6552), 87571,* ☎ ℻ *505/758–5448 or* ☎ *800/758–5448. 9 rooms. Hot tub. Continental breakfast. MC, V.*

$$ 🖬 **El Pueblo Lodge.** This low-to-the-ground, pueblo-style adobe a few blocks north of the Taos Plaza has practical in-room amenities and guest laundry rooms. The traditional Southwestern furnishings and fireplaces lend the rooms a homey feel. ⊠ *412 Paseo del Pueblo Norte (Box 92), 87571,* ☎ *505/758–8700 or 800/433–9612,* FAX *505/ 758–7321. 60 rooms. Kitchenettes, refrigerators, pool, hot tub. Continental breakfast. AE, D, MC, V.*

$$ 🖬 **Hotel La Fonda de Taos.** The La Fonda, once a place of pride in town, was becoming a little ratty looking as the 1990s were drawing to a close. As we went to press, renovations were under way (to be completed during 1999) to restore some of this landmark's luster. ⊠ *Taos Plaza (Box 1447), 87571,* ☎ *505/758–2211 or 800/833–2211,* FAX *505/ 758–8508. 24 rooms. Lounge. AE, MC, V.*

$$ 🖬 **Orinda.** Built in 1947, this is an adobe estate with spectacular views and country privacy. The one- and two-bedroom suites have separate entrances, kiva-style fireplaces, traditional viga ceilings, and Mexican-tile baths. Two rooms share a sitting room. The thick adobe walls ensure peace and quiet. The hearty breakfast is served family-style in the soaring two-story sun atrium amid a gallery of artworks, all for sale. ⊠ *461 Valverde (Box 4451), 87571,* ☎ *505/ 758–8581 or 800/847–1837,* FAX *505/751–4895. 4 rooms. Full breakfast. No smoking. AE, D, MC, V.*

$$ 🖬 **Sagebrush Inn.** A tad run-down but still with a certain allure, this Pueblo-Mission style 1929 adobe 3 mi south of the Plaza contains authentic Navajo rugs, rare pottery, Southwestern and Spanish antiques, fine carved pieces, and paintings by Southwestern masters. Georgia O'Keeffe once lived and painted in one of the third-story rooms. Many of the bedrooms have kiva-style fireplaces; some have balconies looking out to the Sangre de Cristo Mountains. The Sagebrush Village offers condominium family lodging, too. ⊠ *1508 Paseo del Pueblo Sur (Box 557), 87571,* ☎ *505/ 758–2254 or 800/428–3626,* FAX *505/758–5077. 100 rooms and suites. 2 restaurants, lounge, pool, 2 hot tubs. AE, D, DC, MC, V.*

$$ 🖬 **Sun God Lodge.** Though inexpensive, this motel has old adobe charm with basic amenities—it's a good deal. Right on the main highway, the Sun God is convenient to restaurants and historic sites. ⊠ *909 Paseo del Pueblo Sur, 87571,*

☎ 505/758–3162 or 800/821–2437, ⅎⅩ 505/758–1716.
55 rooms. Hot tub. AE, D, MC, V.

Ranchos de Taos

$$$–   🏨 **Adobe & Pines.** Native American and Mexican artifacts
$$$$ decorate the main house of this B&B, which has expansive
views of Taos Mountain. The rooms contain gorgeous
Mexican-tiled baths, kiva fireplaces, fluffy goose-down
pillows, and comforters. A separate cottage and two equally
handsome casitas also house guests. The owners serve
gourmet breakfasts in a sunny glass-enclosed patio. ⊠ *NM
68 and Llano Quemado (Box 837), 87557,* ☎ *505/751–
0947 or 800/723–8267,* ⅎⅩ *505/758–8423. 5 rooms, 1 cot-
tage, 2 casitas. 5 hot tubs, sauna. Full breakfast. No
smoking. AE, MC, V.*

The Enchanted Circle

$$$$ 🏨 **Inn at Snakedance.** This modern, spotlessly clean resort
hotel epitomizes the rustic tradition of European Alpine
lodges. Right on the slopes, the inn has a handsome library
where guests can enjoy an après-ski coffee or after-dinner
drink next to a fieldstone fireplace. The dining room has
a soaring ceiling with 100-year-old beams originally cut for
the copper mines down the road. The rooms, some of them
with fireplaces, have a Southwestern feel. In summer the
hotel offers weeklong vacation packages, including a cook-
ing school and fitness adventure courses. ⊠ *Off Taos Ski
Valley Rd. (County Rd. 150; Box 89), Taos Ski Valley
87525,* ☎ *505/776–2277 or 800/322–9815,* ⅎⅩ *505/776–
1410. 60 rooms. Minibars, refrigerators, hot tub, massage,
sauna, exercise room. AE, DC, MC, V. Closed mid-Apr.–
Memorial Day.*

$$$$ 🏨 **Quail Ridge Inn Resort.** On the way to the Taos Ski Val-
ley, this large resort has one- and two-story modern adobe
bungalows that are comfy and efficient. Some suites have
kitchens. The resort provides a host of recreational ameni-
ties, from organized trail rides to hot-tub soaks. Skiing, ten-
nis, rafting, mountain-biking, and fly-fishing packages are
available. ⊠ *Taos Ski Valley Rd. (County Rd. 150; Box 707),
Taos 87571,* ☎ *505/776–2211 or 800/624–4448,* ⅎⅩ *505/*

776–2949. *110 rooms and suites. Restaurant, lounge, pool, hot tub, 8 tennis courts, exercise room, racquetball, squash, volleyball. AE, D, DC, MC, V.*

$$$ ✕🏠 **Austing Haus.** Owner Paul Austing constructed much ★ of this handsome building 1½ mi from the Taos Ski Valley, along with many of its furnishings. The dining room has large picture windows, stained-glass paneling, a fireplace, and a Native American loom with a partially completed blanket mounted on the wall. Guest rooms are pretty and quiet with harmonious, peaceful colors; some have four-poster beds and fireplaces. The specialties at the restaurant are veal Oscar and steak au poivre. During the winter the inn offers ski packages. ⊠ *Taos Ski Valley Rd. (County Rd. 150; Box 8), Taos Ski Valley 87525, ☎ 505/776–2649, 505/776–2629, or 800/748–2932, ₣AX 505/776–8751. 44 rooms, 3 chalets. Restaurant, hot tub. AE, DC, MC, V.*

$$$ 🏠 **The Bavarian.** A luxurious secluded hideaway, this au-★ thentic re-creation of a Bavarian ski lodge has the only mid-mountain accommodations in the Taos Ski Valley. The King Ludwig suite has a dining room, a kitchenette, a huge marble-tiled bathroom, and two bedrooms with canopied beds. The Lola Montez has a bedroom plus a loft and is a favorite with honeymooners. Three suites have whirlpool tubs, and there's a three-bedroom, three-bath apartment. The restaurant serves Bavarian cuisine and has a comprehensive wine list. Summer activities at the Bavarian include hiking, touring with the resident botanist, horseback riding, rafting, and fishing. Seven-day packages, including two meals a day, range from $1,500 to $1,700 per person. ⊠ *Twining Rd. off County Rd. 150, Taos Ski Valley 87525, ☎ 505/751–6661, ₣AX 505/776–1248. 4 suites. Restaurant, in-room VCRs, kitchenettes, no-smoking rooms. Full breakfast. AE, D, MC, V. Closed May and Oct.*

$$$ 🏠 **Thunderbird Lodge and Chalets.** Only 150 yards from the main lifts, on the sunny side of the Taos Ski Valley, this two-story wood-frame inn is nothing fancy, but it's great for families with kids. A large conference room doubles as a games room, with board games and a library. Supervised children's activities include early dinners, movies, and games. Lodge rooms are small and functional; the rooms in the Chalet are larger and have king-size beds. ⊠ *3 Thunderbird Rd., off Taos Ski Valley Rd. (County Rd. 150; Box*

87), Taos Ski Valley 87525, ☎ 505/776–2280 or 800/
776–2279, ⨋ 505/776–2238. 32 rooms. Restaurant, bar,
hot tub, massage, sauna, conference room. AE, MC, V.

$$$ 🏨 **Touchstone Inn.** D. H. Lawrence visited this house when
★   Miriam DeWitt owned it in 1929. The inn's owner, Taos artist
Bren Price, has filled the rooms, named after famous Taos
literary figures, with tasteful antique and modern pieces.
The grounds overlook part of the Taos Pueblo lands, and this
makes for a quiet stay. Some suites have fireplaces. Early morn-
ing coffee is poured in the living room, and gourmet break-
fasts with inventive presentations are served in the glassed-in
patio. ⊠ 0110 Mabel Dodge La. (Box 2896), Taos 87571,
☎ 505/758–0192 or 800/758–0192, ⨋ 505/758–3498. 8
rooms. In-room VCRs, hot tub. Full breakfast. MC, V.

$$–$$$ 🏨 **Hacienda del Sol.** Art patron Mabel Dodge Luhan
★   bought this house in the 1920s and lived here with her fourth
husband, Tony Luhan, while building their main house, Las
Palomas de Taos. It was also their guest house for visiting
notables; Frank Waters wrote *People of the Valley* here. Most
of the rooms contain kiva-style fireplaces, Spanish an-
tiques, Southwestern-style handcrafted furniture, and orig-
inal artwork. The secluded outdoor hot tub has a crystalline
view of Taos Mountain. The jet-black bathroom of Los
Amantes Room is a celebration in decadence with its huge
black hot tub amid a jungle of potted plants and below a
skylight through which you can gaze at the stars. Break-
fast is a gourmet affair. ⊠ 109 Mabel Dodge La. (Box 177),
Taos 87571, ☎ 505/758–0287, ⨋ 505/758–5895. 10
rooms. Outdoor hot tub. Full breakfast. MC, V.

Campgrounds

🏕 **Carson National Forest.** Within the forest are 30 camp-
sites along 400 mi of cool mountain trout streams and
lakes. You may also choose your own site, anywhere along
a forest road. Contact the U.S. Forest Service for the latest
camping information. ⊠ Forest Service Building, 208 Cruz
Alta Rd., Taos 87571, ☎ 505/758–6200. 30 RV and tent
sites. Rest rooms.

🏕 **Orilla Verde Recreation Area.** You can hike, fish, and
picnic at this area along the Rio Grande, 10 mi south of

Taos. ✉ *Bureau of Land Management, Cruz Alta Rd., Taos 87571,* ☎ *505/758–8851. 70 tent sites. Rest rooms.*

⚠ **Questa Lodge.** This campground is off the Enchanted Circle, 2 blocks from NM 522. The sites are on the Red River. ✉ *Lower Embargo Rd. (Box 155), Questa 87556,* ☎ *505/586–0300 or 800/459–0300. 26 RV sites. Rest rooms, hot showers, basketball, croquet, volleyball, playground, coin laundry. Closed mid-Oct.–Apr.*

⚠ **Roadrunner Campground.** The Red River runs right through this woodsy mountain campground. ✉ *NM 578 (Box 588), Red River 87558,* ☎ *505/754–2286 or 800/ 243–2286. 155 RV sites. Rest rooms, hot showers, grocery, tennis court, video games, playground, laundry, meeting room. Closed mid-Dec.–early spring.*

⚠ **Taos RV Park.** The sites are grassy, with a few small trees, in this park 3½ mi from Taos Plaza near the junction of NM 68 and NM 518. ✉ *1799 Paseo del Pueblo Sur, next to the Taos Motel (Box 729F), Ranchos de Taos 87557,* ☎ *505/758–1667 or 800/323–6009. 29 RV and tent sites. Rest rooms, hot showers, horseshoes, video games, playground.*

NIGHTLIFE AND THE ARTS

Evening entertainment is a modest affair in Taos. Some motels and hotels present solo musicians or small combos in their bars and lounges. Everything from down-home blues bands to Texas two-step dancing blossoms on Saturday and Sunday nights in winter. In summer things heat up during the week as well. For information about what's going on around town pick up *Taos Magazine*. The weekly *Taos News*, published on Thursday, carries arts and entertainment information in the "Tempo" section.

Nightlife

Bars and Lounges

The **Adobe Bar** (✉ Taos Inn, 125 Paseo del Pueblo Norte, ☎ 505/758–2233), a local meet-and-greet spot, books talented acts, from a flute choir to individual guitarists and small jazz, folk, and country bands. **Fernando's Hideaway**

(⊠ Holiday Inn, 1005 Paseo del Pueblo Sur, ☎ 505/758–4444) occasionally presents live entertainment—rock, jazz, blues, vocals, and country music. Saturday is reserved for karaoke. Lavish complimentary happy-hour buffets are laid out on weekday evenings.

Cabaret
The **Kachina Lodge Cabaret** (⊠ 413 Paseo del Pueblo Norte, ☎ 505/758–2275) brings in headline acts, such as Arlo Guthrie and the Kingston Trio, on a regular basis and has dancing.

Coffeehouses
Caffe Tazza (⊠ 122 Kit Carson Rd., ☎ 505/758–8706) presents free evening performances throughout the week—folk singing, poetry readings, open-mike nights, and more.

Country-and-Western Clubs
The **Sagebrush Inn** (⊠ 1508 Paseo del Pueblo Sur, ☎ 505/758–2254) hosts musicians and dancing in its lobby lounge. There's no cover charge, and if you show up on a Thursday, you can learn to two-step.

Jazz Clubs
Thunderbird Lodge (⊠ 3 Thunderbird Rd., ☎ 505/776–2280) in the Taos Ski Valley has free jazz nights. The Thunderbird Jazz Trio performs every Sunday. On Wednesday the lodge brings in a more modern group called Groove Junkies.

The Arts

The **Taos Art Association** (⊠ 133 Paseo del Pueblo Norte, ☎ 505/758–2052) has information about art-related events in Taos. The **Taos Community Auditorium** (⊠ 145 Paseo del Pueblo Norte, ☎ 505/758–4677) presents plays, dance, concerts, and movies.

Festivals
For information about festivals in Taos, contact the **Taos County Chamber of Commerce** (☞ Visitor Information *in* Taos A to Z, *below*).

The **Taos Spring Arts Festival,** held throughout Taos in early May, is a showcase for the visual, performing, and literary arts of the community and allows you to rub elbows with the many artists who call Taos home. The **Taos Fall Arts Festival,** from late September to early October, is the major arts gathering, when buyers are in town and many other events, such as a Taos Pueblo feast, take place. Also in late September is the **Wool Festival,** held in Kit Carson Memorial Park, which celebrates everything from sheep to shawl, with demonstrations of shearing, spinning, and weaving, handmade woolen items for sale, and tastings of favorite lamb dishes.

Film

Taos Talking Picture Festival (☎ 505/751–0637) is a multicultural celebration of cinema artists, with a focus on Native American film and video makers. The mid-April festival presents independent films, documentaries, animation, and some classic cinema.

Music

From mid-June to early August the Taos School of Music and the International Institute of Music fill the evenings with the sounds of chamber and symphonic orchestras at the **Taos Chamber Music Festival** (☎ 505/776–2388). More than three decades old, this is America's oldest summer-music program and possibly the largest assembly of professional musicians in the Southwest. Concerts are presented every Saturday evening from mid-June to August at the Taos Community Auditorium (☞ *above*). Tickets cost $12.

The Taos School of Music gives free weekly summer concerts and recitals from mid-June to early August at the **Hotel Saint Bernard** (☎ 505/776–2251), at the mountain base (near the lifts) of the Taos Ski Valley. **Music from Angel Fire** (☎ 505/758–4667 or 505/377–3233) is a series of classical and jazz concerts presented at the Taos Community Auditorium (☞ *above*) and the Angel Fire Community Auditorium (✉ Town center) from August 21 to September 2. Tickets cost about $12 per concert.

OUTDOOR ACTIVITIES AND SPORTS

Whether you plan to cycle around town, jog along Paseo del Pueblo Norte, or play a few rounds of golf, keep in mind that the altitude in Taos is over 7,000 ft. It's best to keep physical exertion to a minimum until your body becomes acclimated to the altitude—a full day to a few days depending on your constitution. With the decreased oxygen and decreased humidity you may experience some or all of the following symptoms: headaches, nausea, insomnia, shortness of breath, diarrhea, sleeplessness, and tension. If you are planning to engage in physical activity, avoid alcohol and coffee (which aggravate "high-altitude syndrome") and drink a lot of water and juice.

Participant Sports

Bicycling

The Taos-area roads are steep and hilly, and none have marked bicycle lanes, so be careful while cycling. The **Enchanted Circle Wheeler Peak Bicycle Rally** (☎ 800/384–6444) takes place in mid-September. The rally loops through the entire 84-mi Enchanted Circle, through Red River, Taos, Angel Fire, Eagle Nest, and Questa, past a brilliant blaze of fall color. **"Gearing Up" Bicycle Shop** (⊠ 129 Paseo del Pueblo Sur, ☎ 505/751–0365) is a full-service bike shop that also has information about tours and guides.

Hot Tracks (⊠ 214 Paseo del Pueblo Sur, ☎ 505/751–0949) is where the Taos Cycle Club meets. The staff sells all kinds of bikes and is knowledgeable about the best places to go.

Fishing

Picurís Pueblo (☞ Ranchos de Taos and Points South, *in* Exploring Taos, *above*) and Cabresto Lake in the Carson National Forest (☞ Questa *in* The Enchanted Circle, *above*) have good trout fishing. The Upper Red River valley is good for bait and fly fishing. For trout fishing far off the beaten path try Hopewell Lake, in the Carson National Forest, 30 minutes by car from Tre Piedras (35 mi west of Taos). The lake is open from May to October.

Golf

The 18-hole, par-72 course at the **Angel Fire Country Club** (⊠ Country Club Dr. off NM 434, Angel Fire, ☎ 505/377–

3055), one of the highest in the nation, is open from May to mid-October. The greens fee is $35; an optional cart costs $12.50 per person. The greens fee at the 18-hole, par-72 championship course at **Taos Country Club** (⊠ Hwy. 570, Rancho de Taos, ☎ 505/758–7300) ranges between $25 and $42; optional carts cost $22.

Health Clubs

The **Northside Health & Fitness Center** (⊠ 1307 Paseo del Pueblo Norte, ☎ 505/751–1242) is a spotlessly clean facility with indoor and outdoor pools, a hot tub, tennis courts, and aerobics classes. Nonmembers pay $9 per day; passes for a week or longer are also available. The center provides paid child care with a certified Montessori teacher.

Jogging

The track around the football field at **Taos High School** (⊠ 134 Cervantes St., ☎ 505/758–5230) isn't officially open to the public, but no one seems to object when nonstudents jog there. The paths through **Kit Carson Memorial Park** (☞ Taos Plaza and Bent Street *in* Exploring Taos, *above*) make for a pleasant ride. The mountain roads north of Taos present a formidable challenge.

River Rafting

White-water rafting through the wild and scenic Rio Grande is a growing sport in the region. The **Bureau of Land Management Taos Resource Area Office** (☎ 505/758–8851) has a list of registered river guides and information about running the river on your own.

Far Flung Adventures (☎ 800/359–2627 outside Taos, 505/758–2628 in town) operates half-day, full-day, and overnight rafting trips along the Rio Grande and the Rio Chama. **Los Rios River Runners** (☎ 800/544–1181) will take you to your choice of spots—the Rio Chama, the Lower Gorge, or the Taos Box.

Skiing

RESORTS

The five ski resorts within 90 mi of Taos have beginning, intermediate, and advanced slopes and snowmobile and cross-country skiing trails. All the resorts have fine accommodations and safe child-care programs at reasonable prices.

Angel Fire Resort (⊠ N. Angel Fire Rd. off NM 434, Angel Fire, ☎ 505/377–6401; 800/633–7463 outside NM) has a hotel and is open from mid-December to the first week in April. **Red River Ski Area** (⊠ Pioneer Rd. off NM 38, Red River, ☎ 505/754–2382) is open from Thanksgiving to Easter. **Sipapu Lodge and Ski Area** (⊠ NM 518, Vadito, ☎ 505/587–2240) is open from mid-December to the end of March. **Ski Rio** (⊠ NM 196 off NM 522, Costillo, ☎ 505/758–7707), north of the Taos Ski Valley, opens for daily business from mid-December to early April. The resort has 83 runs and makes its own snow. **Taos Ski Valley** (⊠ Taos Ski Valley Rd./County Rd. 150, Taos Ski Valley 87525, ☎ 505/776–2291, 800/776–1111 or 505/776–2233 for reservations, FAX 505/776–8596) is open from late November until the first week in April.

CROSS-COUNTRY

At the **Enchanted Forest Cross-Country Ski Area** (⊠ Box 521, Red River 87558, ☎ 505/754–2374) the season runs from the end of November to Easter. The **Carson National Forest** (⊠ Forest Service Building, 208 Cruz Alta Rd., Taos 87571, ☎ 505/758–6200) has a good self-guided map of cross-country trails throughout the park.

Swimming

The **Don Fernando Municipal Swimming Pool** (⊠ 124 Civic Plaza Dr., ☎ 505/758–9171) is open on weekdays from 1 to 4:30 and on weekends from 1 to 5. The admission charge is $2.

Tennis

Fred Baca Park (⊠ 301 Camino de Medio) and **Kit Carson Memorial Park** (⊠ Paseo del Pueblo Norte at Civic Plaza Dr.) have free public tennis courts, available on a first-come, first-served basis. The **Quail Ridge Inn and Tennis Ranch** (⊠ Taos Ski Valley Rd./County Rd. 150, ☎ 800/624–4448) has eight Laykold tennis courts (two indoor), which are free to guests and cost $30 per hour (indoor courts) for visitors. Each summer the resort offers tennis programs with Tim Cass, the head coach of the University of New Mexico's Men's Tennis Team.

Spectator Sports

Spectator sports in the Taos area include the **Rodeo de Taos,** which takes place at the Taos County Fairgrounds in mid-June, and the **Taos Mountain Balloon Rally,** held in a field south of downtown during the last week in October in conjunction with the "Taste of Taos" food and wine tasting. Contact the Taos County Chamber of Commerce (☞ Visitor Information *in* Taos A to Z, *below*) for more information.

SHOPPING

Shopping Districts

Taos Plaza consists mostly of T-shirt emporiums and souvenir shops that are easily bypassed, though a few stores, like Blue Rain Gallery, carry quality Native American artifacts and jewelry. The more upscale galleries and boutiques are two short blocks north on Bent Street. Kit Carson Road, also known as U.S. 64, has a mix of the old and the new. There's metered municipal parking downtown, though the traffic can be daunting. Some shops worth checking out are in St. Francis Plaza, 4 mi south of the Plaza near the San Francisco de Asís Church.

Galleries

Blue Rain Gallery (⊠ 115 Taos Plaza, ☎ 505/751–0066) carries some of the finest examples of Pueblo pottery and Hopi kachina dolls to be found anywhere, ranging in price from several hundred to several thousand dollars. The owner, Leroy Garcia, takes time to explain the materials and traditions; you'll learn a great deal during a short visit here. The gallery also sells Indian-made jewelry and art.

Carol Savid Gallery (⊠ 103B Bent St., ☎ 505/758–1128) displays the artist's luminous sculptural, architectural, and functional glass pieces, all created with dichroic glass.

Clay and Fiber Gallery (⊠ 126 W. Plaza, ☎ 505/758–8093), on the southwestern corner of the Plaza, exhibits the first-rate ceramics, glass, pottery, and hand-painted silks and weavings of many local artists.

El Taller Taos Gallery (✉ 237 Ledoux St., ☎ 505/758–4887) is the exclusive representative of Amado Peña, a Southwestern artist who works in various media. The gallery also exhibits sculpture, jewelry, weavings, glass, and clay.

Fenix Gallery (✉ 228B Paseo del Pueblo Norte, ☎ 505/758–9120), a showcase for contemporary art, exhibits paintings, sculpture, ceramics, and lithography, along with antique Latin American textiles.

Franzetti Metalworks (✉ 120G Bent St., ☎ 505/758–7872) displays the owner Pozzi Franzetti's metalwork creations—from sophisticated sculptures to sprightly wall hangings in Western motifs.

Lumina Gallery (✉ 239 Morada La., ☎ 505/758–7282), inside the former adobe home of Victor Higgins, one of the original members of the Taos Society of Artists, exhibits contemporary art—paintings, sculpture, photography, and jewelry. The sculpture garden is a serene oasis conducive to lingering, which the owners happily encourage.

Leo Weaver Jewelry Galleries (✉ 62 St. Francis Plaza, Ranchos de Taos, ☎ 505/751–1003; ✉ Taos Inn, 125 Paseo del Pueblo Norte, ☎ 505/758–8171) represents 50 local jewelry artists at two locations. You'll find contemporary and traditional designs in silver, gold, and precious stones, as well as beautiful silver concha belts.

Mission Gallery (✉ 138 E. Kit Carson Rd., ☎ 505/758–2861) carries the works of early Taos artists, early New Mexico modernists, and important contemporary artists. The gallery is in the former home of painter Joseph H. Sharp.

Navajo Gallery (✉ 210 Ledoux St., ☎ 505/758–3250) shows the works of owner and Navajo painter R. C. Gorman, known for his ethereal interpretations of Indian imagery.

R. B. Ravens Gallery (✉ St. Francis Plaza, Ranchos de Taos, ☎ 505/758–7322) exhibits paintings by the founding artists of Taos, pre-1930s weavings, and ceramics.

Shriver Gallery (⊠ 401 Paseo del Pueblo Norte, ☎ 505/758–4994) handles drawings and etchings, traditional bronze sculpture, and paintings, including oils, watercolors, and pastels.

Six Directions (⊠ 110 S. Plaza, ☎ 505/758–4376) exhibits paintings, alabaster and bronze sculpture, Native American artifacts, silver jewelry, and pottery. Bill Rabbit and Robert Redbird are among the artists represented here.

Specialty Stores

Books

Brodsky Bookshop (⊠ 218 Paseo del Pueblo Norte, ☎ 505/758–9468), which carries books and music, has a casual atmosphere. The books—contemporary literature, Southwestern classics, children's titles—are sometimes piled every which way, but the amiable staff will help you find whatever you need.

Fernandez de Taos Book Store (⊠ 109 N. Plaza, ☎ 505/758–4391) carries magazines, major out-of-town newspapers, and books on Southwestern culture and history.

G. Robinson Old Prints and Maps (⊠ John Dunn House, 124D Bent St., ☎ 505/758–2278) stocks rare books, Edward Curtis photographs, and maps and prints from the 16th to 19th centuries.

Merlin's Garden (⊠ 127 Bent St., ☎ 505/758–0985) is a funky repository of metaphysical books and literature from Ram Dass to Thomas More. The shop also carries tapes, incense, crystals, and jewelry.

Moby Dickens (⊠ No. 6, John Dunn House, 124A Bent St., ☎ 505/758–3050), great for browsing, has windows that let in the bright Taos sun. A bookstore for all ages, it carries best-sellers and many books on the Southwest.

Mystery Ink (⊠ 121 Camino de la Placita, ☎ 505/751–1092) specializes in high-quality used books, especially murder mysteries. The shop also carries some foreign-language literature.

Taos Book Shop (⊠ 122D Kit Carson Rd., ☎ 505/758–
3733), the oldest bookshop in New Mexico, founded in
1947, specializes in out-of-print and Southwestern books.
The founders, Genevieve Janssen and Claire Morrill, com-
piled the reminiscences of their Taos years in the interesting *A Taos Mosaic* (University of New Mexico Press). Book
signings and author receptions are frequently held.

Clothing

Mariposa Boutique (⊠ John Dunn House, 120F Bent St.,
☎ 505/758–9028) sells Southwestern clothing and accessories by leading Taos designers. The store also sells handcrafted jewelry.

Overland Sheepskin Company (⊠ NM 522, ☎ 505/758–
8822; 100A McCarthy Plaza, ☎ 505/758–5150) carries
high-quality sheepskin coats, hats, mittens, and slippers,
many with Taos beadwork.

Taos Moccasin Co. Factory Outlet (⊠ 216 Paseo del Pueblo
Sur, ☎ 505/758–4276) sells moccasins made in the building next door—everything from booties for babies to men's
high and low boots. This shop has great discounts and interesting designs.

Home Furnishings

Casa Cristal Pottery (⊠ NM 522, El Prado 87529, ☎ 505/
758–1530), 2½ mi north of the Taos Plaza, has it all:
stoneware, serapes, clay pots, Native American ironwood
carvings, ceramic sunbursts, straw and tin ornaments, fountains, sweaters, ponchos, clay fireplaces, Mexican blankets,
clay churches, birdbaths, baskets, tile, piñatas, and blue glass-
ware from Guadalajara. Also in stock are antique repro-
ductions of park benches, street lamps, mailboxes, bakers'
racks, and other wrought-iron products.

Country Furnishings of Taos (⊠ 534 Paseo del Pueblo
Norte, ☎ 505/758–4633) sells folk art from northern New
Mexico, handmade furniture, metalwork lamps and beds,
and many other colorful accessories for the home.

Flying Carpet (⊠ 208 Ranchitos Rd., ☎ 505/751–4035)
carries colorful rugs and kilims from Turkey, Kurdistan, Per-
sia, and elsewhere. Owner Bill Eagleton, who wrote a book

about Kurdish carpets, and his wife Kay have a keen eye for quality and design.

Hacienda de San Francisco (⊠ 4 St. Francis Plaza, Ranchos de Taos, ☎ 505/758–0477) has an exceptional collection of Spanish-colonial antiques.

Lo Fino (⊠ 201 Paseo del Pueblo Sur, ☎ 505/758–0298) carries the works—hand-carved beds, tables, and chairs—of the 10 top Southwestern furniture and lighting designers, as well as some Native American alabaster sculpture, basketry, and pottery.

Partridge Company (⊠ 241 Ledoux St., at Ranchitos Rd., ☎ 505/758–1225) sells linens, rugs, woven bedcovers, and accessories. The shop's owner fashions some eye-catching dried-flower arrangements.

Taos Blue (⊠ 101A Bent St., ☎ 505/758–3561) specializes in Taos-style interior furnishings. Also here are Pawnee/Sioux magical masks, "storyteller figures" from the Taos Pueblo, ceramic dogs baying at the moon, and Native American shields and rattles, sculpture, leather hassocks, and painted buckskin pillows.

Taos Company (⊠ 124K Bent St., ☎ 800/548–1141) sells magnificent Spanish-style furniture, chandeliers, rugs and textiles, Mexican *equipal* (wood and leather) chairs, and other accessories.

Native American Arts and Crafts

Broken Arrow (⊠ 222 N. Plaza, ☎ 505/758–4304) specializes in collector-quality Native American arts and crafts, including sand paintings, rugs, prints, jewelry, pottery, artifacts, and Hopi kachina dolls.

Buffalo Dancer (⊠ 103A E. Plaza, ☎ 505/758–8718) buys, sells, and trades Native American arts and crafts, including pottery, belts, kachina dolls, and silver-coin jewelry.

Don Fernando Curios and Gifts (⊠ 104 W. Plaza, ☎ 505/758–3791), which opened in 1938 (it's the oldest Native American arts shop on the Taos Plaza), sells good turquoise jewelry, kachinas, straw baskets, and colorful beads.

El Rincón (⊠ 114 E. Kit Carson Rd., ☎ 505/758–9188) is housed in a large, dark, cluttered century-old adobe. Native American items of all kinds are bought and sold here: drums, feathered headdresses, Navajo rugs, beads, bowls, baskets, shields, beaded moccasins, jewelry, arrows, and spearheads. The packed back room contains Indian, Hispanic, and Anglo Wild West artifacts.

Southwest Moccasin & Drum (⊠ 803 Paseo del Pueblo Norte, ☎ 505/758–9332 or 800/447–3630) has one of the country's largest selections: 716 native moccasin styles and 72 sizes of drums, many painted by local artists.

Taos Drums (⊠ Santa Fe Hwy./NM 68, ☎ 505/758–3796 or 800/424–3786) is the factory outlet for the Taos Drum Factory. The store, 5 mi south of the Taos Plaza (look for the large tepee), stocks handmade Pueblo log drums, leather lamp shades, and wrought-iron and Southwest furniture.

Taos General Store (⊠ 233C Paseo del Pueblo Sur, ☎ 505/758–9051) is an airy shop that sells Navajo, Zuñi, and Hopi jewelry and pottery at reasonable prices. There's a small area in the back with Mexican peasant artifacts and home accessories.

TAOS A TO Z

Arriving and Departing

By Bus
Texas, New Mexico & Oklahoma Coaches (☎ 800/231–2222), a subsidiary of Greyhound Lines, runs buses from Albuquerque to Taos. Buses stop at the **Taos Bus Station** (⊠ 1353 Paseo del Pueblo Sur, ☎ 505/758–1144).

By Car
The main route from Santa Fe to Taos is NM 68. From points north of Taos, take NM 522; from points east or west, take U.S. 64. You can also take the scenic High Road to Taos. For a description of the route and the towns along it, *see* Side Trips *in* Chapter 2.

Roads can be treacherously icy during the winter months; call **New Mexico Road Conditions** (☎ 800/432–4269) before heading out. The altitude in Taos will affect your car's performance, causing it to "gasp" because it's getting too much gas and not enough air. If a smooth ride matters, you can have your car tuned up for high-altitude driving.

By Plane
See Air Travel *in* Essential Information.

By Train
Amtrak (☎ 800/872–7245) operates the *Southwest Chief* between Chicago and Los Angeles. The train stops at the **Lamy train station** (✉ County Rd. 41, Lamy 87500), south of Santa Fe and about 88 mi from Taos. **Faust's Transportation** (☎ 505/758–3410 or 505/758–7359) operates radio-dispatched taxis to and from the Lamy station. The *Southwest Chief* also stops in Las Vegas, 78 mi southeast of Taos.

Getting Around

Taos radiates around its central Plaza and is easily maneuvered on foot: Many restaurants, stores, boutiques, and galleries are on or near the Plaza. The main street through town is Paseo del Pueblo (NM 68 downtown).

By Car
Major hotels have ample parking. Metered parking areas are all over town; during the peak seasons—summer and winter—traffic and parking can be a headache. There's a metered parking lot between Taos Plaza and Bent Street.

By Taxi
Taxi service is sparse. However, **Faust's Transportation** (☎ 505/758–3410 or 505/758–7359), based in nearby El Prado, has a fleet of radio-dispatched cabs.

Guided Tours

Orientation
Pride of Taos Tours (☎ 505/758–8340) operates 70-minute narrated trolley tours of Taos highlights, including the San Francisco de Asís Church, Taos Pueblo, and a Taos drum shop. Tours run from May to October and cost $15 each.

Special-Interest

Marisha's Magic Carpet–The Ultimate Concierge (☎ 505/758–3391 or 800/211–8267) will book everything from hotel and restaurant reservations to walking and art tours, hot-air ballooning, and horseback riding. **Native Sons Adventures** (✉ 715 Paseo del Pueblo Sur, Taos, ☎ 505/758–9342 or 800/753–7559) organizes biking, backpacking, rafting, snowmobiling, and horseback expeditions.

Contacts and Resources

B&B Reservation Agency

Taos Bed and Breakfast Association (✉ Box 2772, 87571, ☎ 800/876–7857).

Emergencies

Ambulance, Fire, and **Police** (☎ 911).

New Mexico state police (☎ 505/758–8878). **Taos police** (☎ 505/758–2216). **Holy Cross Hospital** (✉ 630 Paseo del Pueblo Sur, ☎ 505/758–8883).

Pharmacies

Taos Pharmacy (✉ Piñon Plaza, 622A Paseo del Pueblo Sur, ☎ 505/758–3342). **Furr's Pharmacy** (✉ 1100 Paseo del Pueblo Sur, ☎ 505/758–1203). **Wal-Mart Discount Pharmacy** (✉ 926 Paseo de Pueblo Sur, ☎ 505/758–2743).

Visitor Information

Taos County Chamber of Commerce (✉ 1139 Paseo del Pueblo Sur, Drawer 1, Taos 87571, ☎ 505/758–3873 or 800/732–8267).

GLOSSARY

Perhaps more than any other region in the United States, New Mexico has its own distinctive cuisine heavily influenced by Native American, Spanish-colonial, Mexican, and American frontier traditions.

As befits a land occupied—in several senses of the word in some cases—by so many diverse peoples, the use of accents on place and other names is a tricky matter. For some people, among them many Hispanic residents, accents are a matter of identification and pride—Río Grande, for instance, represents more clearly the linguistic origins of the current name of the river that runs so grandly through the state. On the other hand, though including the accent for Picurís Pueblo or Jémez Pueblo might be linguistically accurate, it's also a reminder to a Pueblo Native American of his or her nation's conquest by the Spanish. ("I couldn't care less whether you use accents or not—I don't," said a woman at the governor's office of Jemez Pueblo when asked whether having an accent above the first "e" in the pueblo's name would be more accurate.)

In general in this book we've applied accents when they're part of an official place or other name. Signs for and official documents of Española, for instance, tend to have a tilde above the "n" in the city's name. On the other hand, though the names of Capulin Volcano and the city of Raton are sometimes written Capulín Volcano and Ratón, we have not employed the accents because New Mexican residents rarely do. A generally workable solution, this strategy does leads to some apparent inconsistencies (Picurís Pueblo; Jemez Pueblo), an illustration of the conflicting cultural sentiments still at play within New Mexico.

Menu Guide

Aguacate: Spanish for avocado, the key ingredient of guacamole

Albóndigas: Meatballs, usually cooked with rice in a meat broth

Bolsa del pobre: A seafood and vegetable dish; a specialty from Colima

Burrito: A warm flour tortilla wrapped around meat, beans, and vegetables, and smothered in chile and cheese

Carne adovada: Red chile–marinated pork

Chalupa: A corn tortilla deep-fried in the shape of a bowl, filled with pinto beans (sometimes meat), and topped with cheese, guacamole, sour cream, lettuce, tomatoes, and salsa

Chile relleno: A large green chile pepper peeled, stuffed with cheese or a special mixture of spicy ingredients, dipped in batter, and fried

Chiles: New Mexico's infamous hot peppers, which come in an endless variety of sizes and in various degrees of hotness, from the thumb-size jalapeño to the smaller and often hotter serrano. They can be canned or fresh, dried or cut up into salsa.

Chimichanga: The same as a burrito (☞ *above*) only deep-fried and topped with a dab of sour cream or salsa

Chipotle: A dried smoked jalapeño with a smoky, almost sweet, chocolatey flavor

Chorizo: Well-spiced Spanish sausage, made with pork and red chiles

Enchilada: A rolled or flat corn tortilla filled with meat, chicken, seafood, or cheese, an enchilada is covered with chile and baked. The ultimate enchilada is made with blue Indian corn tortillas. New Mexicans order them flat, sometimes topped with a fried egg.

Fajitas: Grilled beef, chicken, or fish with peppers and onions and served with tortillas; traditionally known as arracheras

Flauta: A tortilla filled with cheese or meat and rolled into a flutelike shape (flauta means flute) and lightly fried.

Frijoles refritos: Refried beans, often seasoned with lard or cheese

Guacamole: Mashed avocado, mixed with tomatoes, garlic, onions, lemon juice, and chiles, used as a dip, a side dish, a topping, or an additional ingredient

Huevos rancheros: New Mexico's answer to eggs Benedict—eggs doused with chile and sometimes melted cheese, served on top of a corn tortilla (they're good accompanied by chorizo)

Pan de cazón: Grilled shark with black beans and red onions on a tortilla; a specialty from Campeche

Posole: Resembling popcorn soup, this is a sublime marriage of lime, hominy, pork, chile, garlic, and spices.

Quesadilla: A folded flour tortilla filled with cheese and meat or vegetables, and warmed or lightly fried so the cheese melts

Queso: Cheese; an ingredient in many Mexican and Southwestern recipes

Ristra: String of dried red chile peppers, often used as decoration

Sopaipilla: Puffy deep-fried bread, served with honey

Taco: A corn or flour tortilla baked or fried and made into a shell that's then stuffed with vegetables or spicy meat and garnished with shredded lettuce, chopped tomatoes, onions, and grated cheese

Tacos al carbón: Shredded pork cooked in a mole sauce and folded into corn tortillas

Tamale: Ground corn made into a dough and filled with finely ground pork and red chiles, then steamed in a corn husk

Tortilla: A thin pancake made of corn or wheat flour, a tortilla is used as bread, as an edible "spoon," and as a container for other foods. Locals place butter in the center of a hot tortilla, roll it up, and eat it as a scroll.

Trucha en terra-cotta: Fresh trout wrapped in corn husks and baked in clay

Verde: Spanish for "green," as in chile verde (a green chile sauce)

INDEX

✕ = restaurant, 🏨 = hotel

NOTES

NOTES

NOTES

Looking for a different kind of vacation?

Fodor's makes it easy with a full line of specialty guidebooks to suit a variety of interests—from sports and adventure to romance to family fun.

At bookstores everywhere.
www.fodors.com

Fodor's Travel Publications

Available at bookstores everywhere. For descriptions of all our titles and a key to Fodor's guidebook series, visit www.fodors.com/books

Gold Guides

U.S.

Alaska	Florida	New York City	Santa Fe, Taos,
Arizona	Hawai'i	Oregon	Albuquerque
Boston	Las Vegas, Reno,	Pacific North	Seattle &
California	Tahoe	Coast	Vancouver
Cape Cod,	Los Angeles	Philadelphia & the	The South
Martha's Vineyard,	Maine, Vermont,	Pennsylvania	U.S. & British
Nantucket	New Hampshire	Dutch Country	Virgin Islands
The Carolinas &	Maui & Lāna'i	The Rockies	USA
Georgia	Miami & the Keys	San Diego	Virginia &
Chicago	New England	San Francisco	Maryland
Colorado	New Orleans		Washington, D.C.

Foreign

Australia	Eastern &	Madrid &	Provence &
Austria	Central Europe	Barcelona	the Riviera
The Bahamas	Europe	Mexico	Scandinavia
Belize &	Florence, Tuscany	Montréal &	Scotland
Guatemala	& Umbria	Québec City	Singapore
Bermuda	France	Moscow,	South Africa
Canada	Germany	St. Petersburg,	South America
Cancún, Cozumel,	Great Britain	Kiev	Southeast Asia
Yucatán Peninsula	Greece	The Netherlands,	Spain
Caribbean	Hong Kong	Belgium &	Sweden
China	India	Luxembourg	Switzerland
Costa Rica	Ireland	New Zealand	Thailand
Cuba	Israel	Norway	Toronto
The Czech	Italy	Nova Scotia, New	Turkey
Republic &	Japan	Brunswick, Prince	Vienna & the
Slovakia	London	Edward Island	Danube Valley
Denmark		Paris	Vietnam
		Portugal	

Special-Interest Guides

Adventures to	Fodor's How to Pack	Healthy Escapes	Rock & Roll
Imagine	Great American	Kodak Guide to	Traveler USA
Alaska Ports of Call	Learning Vacations	Shooting Great	Sunday in San
Ballpark Vacations	Great American	Travel Pictures	Francisco
The Best Cruises	Sports & Adventure	National Parks	Walt Disney
Caribbean Ports	Vacations	and Seashores	World for Adults
of Call	Great American	of the East	Weekends in
The Complete	Vacations	National Parks of	New York
Guide to America's	Great American	the West	Wendy Perrin's
National Parks	Vacations	Nights to Imagine	Secrets Every
Europe Ports of Call	for Travelers	Orlando Like a Pro	Smart Traveler
Family Adventures	with Disabilities	Rock & Roll	Should Know
Fodor's Gay Guide	Halliday's	Traveler Great	Worlds to Imagine
to the USA	New Orleans	Britain and Ireland	
	Food Explorer		

Fodor's Special Series

WHEREVER YOU TRAVEL, *H*ELP IS NEVER FAR AWAY.

From planning your trip to providing travel assistance along the way, American Express® Travel Service Offices are always there to help you do more.

Santa Fe and Taos

Santa Fe
Pajarito Travel (R)
2801 Rodeo Road
Suite B
505/474-7177

do more AMERICAN EXPRESS

Travel
www.americanexpress.com/travel

**American Express Travel Service Offices
are located throughout Santa Fe and Taos.
For the office nearest you, call 1-800-AXP-3429.**